REGULATING SCREENS

Regulating Screens

Issues in Broadcasting and Internet Governance for Children

ANDRÉ H. CARON AND RONALD I. COHEN

With the collaboration of
Marc-André Gauthier, Geneviève Bourret-Roy,
Alexandre Caron, and Pierre-Luc Chabot

McGill-Queen's University Press
Montreal & Kingston • London • Ithaca

ISBN 978-0-7735-4209-9 (cloth)
ISBN 978-0-7735-4210-5 (paper)
ISBN 978-0-7735-8921-6 (ePDF)
ISBN 978-0-7735-8922-3 (ePUB)

Legal deposit third quarter 2013
Bibliothèque nationale du Québec

This book is derived from an edition first published in French as *Les enfants et leurs écrans*

Printed in Canada on acid-free paper that is 100% ancient forest free (100% post-consumer recycled), processed chlorine free.

McGill-Queen's University Press acknowledges the support of the Canada Council for the Arts for our publishing program. We also acknowledge the financial support of the Government of Canada through the Canada Book Fund for our publishing activities.

Library and Archives Canada Cataloguing in Publication

Caron, André H.
[Enfants et leurs écrans. English]
Regulating screens : issues in broadcasting and internet governance for children / André H. Caron and Ronald I. Cohen, with the collaboration of Marc-André Gauthier, Geneviève Bourret-Roy, Alexandre Caron, and Pierre-Luc Chabot.

Originally published in French under title: Enfants et leurs écrans.
Includes bibliographical references and index.
Issued in print and electronic formats.
ISBN 978-0-7735-4209-9 (bound). – ISBN 978-0-7735-4210-5 (pbk.) – ISBN 978-0-7735-8921-6 (ePDF). – ISBN 978-0-7735-8922-3 (ePUB)

1. Children's television programs – Government policy – Canada. 2. Children's television programs – Safety regulations – Canada. 3. Internet and children – Government policy – Canada. 4. Internet and children – Safety regulations – Canada. I. Cohen, Ronald I., author II. Title. III. Title: Enfants et leurs écrans. English.

PN1992.8.C46C37413 2013 791.45083'0971 C2013-902514-6
C2013-902515-4

This book was typeset by True to Type in 10.5/13.5 Sabon

Contents

Acknowledgments

We would like to express our gratitude to all those who assisted us with the research for and preparation of this book, and to those who participated in the evolution of the underlying material. These include Marc-André Gauthier, Geneviève Bourret-Roy, and Alexandre Caron, who were especially involved in the preliminary French version of the work, *Les enfants et leurs écrans* (Presses de l'Université de Montréal, 2011), from which the present book was derived, as well as Teisha Gaylard and John MacNab, major participants in the growth and evolution of self-regulatory principles in Canadian television (and radio), who also responded to our numerous queries as needed during the writing of the book. We are especially indebted to Pierre-Luc Chabot and Ninozka Marrder for their assistance and to Mary Baker for her professional services in the translation and adaptation of the original French text.

Acronyms

AAP	American Association of Pediatrics
ACA	Association of Canadian Advertisers
ACCM	Australian Council on Children and Media
ACMA	Australian Communications and Media Authority
AGVOT	Action Group on Violence on Television
APFTQ	Association des producteurs de films et de télévision du Québec
ASA	Advertising Standards Authority
ASC	Advertising Standards Canada
ASP	Association of Shareware Professionals
BBM	Bureau of Broadcast Measurement (BBM Canada since 2001)
BPCPA	Business Practices and Consumer Protection Authority (British Columbia)
CAAB	Canadian Advertising Advisory Board
CAB	Canadian Association of Broadcasters
CAF	Canadian Advertising Foundation
CAIP	Canadian Association of Internet Providers
CBC	Canadian Broadcasting Corporation
CBSC	Canadian Broadcast Standards Council
CCA	Concerned Children's Advertisers
CCCP	Canadian Centre for Child Protection
CCTA	Canadian Cable Television Association
CDA	Communication Decency Act (1996)
CEFRIO	Centre francophone d'informatisation des organisations
CFTPA	Canadian Film and Television Production Association

CHVRS Canadian Home Video Rating System
CMA Canadian Marketing Association
CMPA Canadian Media Production Association
CMPDA Canadian Motion Picture Distributors Association
COPPA Children's Online Privacy Protection Act (1998)
CRTC Canadian Radio-television and Telecommunications Commission
CSA Conseil supérieur de l'audiovisuel
CYMS Centre for Youth and Media Studies
ESA Entertainment Software Association
ESAC Entertainment Software Association of Canada
ESRB Entertainment Software Rating Board
ESRBi Entertainment Software Rating Board Interactive
FCC Federal Communications Commission (US)
FOSI Family Online Safety Institute
FTC Federal Trade Commission (US)
GSMA The GSM (Groupe spéciale mobile) Association
ICA Institute of Communications and Advertising
ICRA Internet Content Rating Association
IIA Internet Industry Association (Australia)
IDSA Interactive Digital Software Association
INHOPE International Association of Internet Hotlines
IRTE Institut de radio télévision pour enfants (Children's Broadcast Institute)
MPA Motion Picture Association – Canada
NARC National Advertising Review Council
NGO Non-governmental organization
Ofcom Office of Communications (UK)
OPC Office de la protection du consommateur (Quebec)
PPV Pay-per-view television services
RCC Retail Council of Canada
RCMP Royal Canadian Mounted Police
RSAC Recreational Software Advisory Council
SCN Saskatchewan Communications Network
SPA Software Publishers Association
SRC Société Radio-Canada
TFO French-language educational/cultural television channel
TVO TVOntario, English-language television channel

UCLA	The University of California, Los Angeles
VMC	Violence in the Media Coalition
VOD	Video on demand
VRC	Videogame Rating Council
YMA	Youth Media Alliance
YTV	English-language specialty channel aimed at youth

Foreword

There is no doubt that today's children and teens live in a media-saturated world, one where it is not unusual for them to spend close to eight hours a day in front of various screens.[1] And when children interact with media – whether by watching television, surfing the Internet, or listening to music on their iPods – they absorb a large portion of their knowledge about the world and their perceptions of themselves and others.

With this in mind, Canadian governments, regulatory agencies, and industry associations have developed a number of rules and tools to ensure quality children's programming and to safeguard children's and youths' physical and emotional well-being in their media lives. Understanding the laws and regulations that govern Canadian media – and the reasoning behind them – is increasingly important in an era of rapidly changing media platforms where content falls outside the reach of existing regulatory frameworks and transcends national borders.

The convergence of media platforms and the availability of mobile communications technologies mean that rating and classification systems, legislation, and industry codes and guidelines no longer suffice to protect children – particularly in the light of their growing use of mobile devices to access video games, television programs, movies, and music. For this reason, understanding the media issues children face is part of parenting and teaching in a digital world, as is knowing how to provide them with the critical thinking skills they need to be thoughtful and engaged users of all media.

In this comprehensive and informative book, André H. Caron and Ronald I. Cohen track the regulatory path that has defined and established the industry standards for children's and youths' programming in Canada. Through their study of the media issues such regulation strives to address, such as stereotyping and equitable portrayal, violence, advertising and classification systems, as well as the principal stakeholders involved in decision-making processes, the authors provide a deeper understanding of "Canadian values" as they pertain to children and media, and of various stakeholders' roles in defining them. This knowledge is essential for maintaining high standards in today's difficult global digital media landscape as society strives to balance access and legislation with the needs of Canadian families and their children – topics that Caron and Cohen address in their chapter on the Internet.

The challenges within this landscape are huge, especially since the laws and regulations that apply to Canadian broadcasters do not apply to Internet providers. (Moreover, children access networked devices at increasingly young ages.) How does society protect children in a digital sphere where there are no content standards or watersheds, age restrictions on websites are easy to circumvent, and personal information is vulnerable? Can we continue to rely on the traditional self-regulatory models that have been the mainstay of Canadian broadcasting guidelines? What additional issues should we address? Which additional stakeholders need to be involved? These are key questions that the authors bring forward in *Regulating Screens: Issues in Broadcasting and Internet Governance for Children*.

In the new media landscape, young people constantly travel virtually without regard for, and indeed well beyond, geographic and regulatory borders to access media content, and so the responsibility to protect them necessarily shifts to individual households, schools, and communities. Parents and teachers understand they have a significant role to play in helping children learn to think critically about media content. In research at MediaSmarts, 88 per cent of teachers and 91 per cent of parents reported they are most responsible for helping children learn to think critically about what they hear, read, and see in media.[2] But they cannot do this alone; they need digital and media literacy tools and resources for support.

When it comes to the Internet, there is considerable talk about the impact of digital literacy and life skills on Canada's economy and society. Digital literacy was a pillar of the Canadian government's digital economy consultation process in 2010, and a 2011 Canadian Radio-television Telecommunications Commission (CRTC)-sponsored paper on convergence trends notes, "Governing bodies and regulators have a role to play in promoting digital literacy and encouraging citizens to access and utilize digital information, communications, and technologies."[3]

Despite the rhetoric, there is no coordinated effort between government, industry, and education to support digital and media literacy – which means that Canada, once a pioneer in this field, is falling behind many other countries. But there is one advantage in being last out of the gate, namely, having the opportunity to learn from the precedents and best practices created in other countries. To this end, the various legislative, regulatory, and educational approaches that have been put in place in the European Union, the United States, and Australia can only help to inform the process here in Canada.

As *Regulating Screens* so ably illustrates, media are constantly evolving, necessitating in turn the evolution of our responses – especially when it comes to children and youth. My organization, MediaSmarts, is a good example of this. It grew out of the CRTC's television violence initiative in the early 1990s and was originally conceptualized as a clearing house for resources on media violence. At that time, the CRTC's policy on this issue insisted that, although industry codes, classification systems, and technology would play a role, public awareness and media literacy programs were the primary way to address the portrayal of violence in media, especially on television. Not long after MediaSmarts' creation, a broader need for educational resources was recognized on a wide range of media issues and media (including the then newly mainstream Internet), and its mandate expanded accordingly.

In their conclusion, Caron and Cohen highlight educated and engaged parents as a significant piece of the regulatory puzzle. There is no doubt that media-literate individuals are better able to interpret and value media content and understand its cultural, political, commercial, and social implications. More importantly, media-literate parents and teachers are essential in showing children and youth that they have a voice and a role to play as active media consumers, and that they can talk to the entertainment industries and express their opinions through the existing Canadian mechanisms to address media content issues. *Regulating Screens* is an important tool to help the media-concerned, the media-literate, and the media-learners do this.

Jane Tallim
January 2013

REGULATING SCREENS

Introduction

Whatever hesitations are expressed from time to time about the possible harm to free speech that can result from restricting either broadcast or Internet content for the "greater good," people generally coalesce around the good of children. There appears to be general rallying to justify protecting children from content that may harm them, despite the inevitable concomitant restriction on freedom of expression.

It is, therefore, not surprising to see this somewhat universal concern for children's well-being at the root of legislative, regulatory, and self-regulatory measures that target the emerging, as well as traditional, media we will discuss in the following pages. In Canada, the collective societal will to protect children has resulted in mechanisms designed to limit their exposure to inappropriate content on television and film. However, governments, regulators, industry, and educators are still taking the first shaky steps towards establishing frames of reference for new media.

The primordial right to freedom of expression has fundamental constitutional status. The Canadian Charter of Rights and Freedoms states that all Canadian legislation must be consistent with its guaranteed freedoms, which may be restricted only insofar as judged reasonable and justifiable in a free and democratic society. While, in the technical legal sense, the charter does not apply to self-regulatory codes, rules, and standards, its supra-legal role influences all legislative and regulatory measures.

In this book, we focus primarily on Canada's broadcasting regulations. Due to Canada's constitutional framework, the federal parliament has exclusive jurisdiction over broadcasting and competition law, while the provincial legislatures exercise jurisdiction over advertising, the cinema, and the distribution of home video products. By their nature, self-regulatory measures, adopted by and imposed on members of industry and their associations, easily cross over jurisdictional lines without legal consequence.

While self-regulatory standards are, in principle, voluntary and without direct punitive consequences, they occasionally carry authority and, consequently, importance. Government laws and regulation are, by definition, binding, although the nature of the penalties may vary. In Canada, the Canadian Radio-television Telecommunications Commission (CRTC) has the supreme authority to issue, renew, vary, or refuse to renew broadcasting licences although, unlike the American Federal Communications Commission (FCC), the French Conseil supérieur de l'audiovisuel (CSA), or the British Office of Communications (Ofcom), the CRTC does not have the power to impose administrative monetary penalties.

Although our primary focus in this book is on Canadian regulation and self-regulation, with the advent of globalization, we also touch on the issue of new media and children at the international level.

Few publications have synthesized primary data on Canadian regulation and self-regulation specifically concerning children and the various forms of audiovisual content to which they are exposed, which is now principally digital.[1] Compiling the relevant regulatory and self-regulatory texts in this area is a difficult task because many of the protective measures fall outside of the public legislative and regulatory record. Indeed, one might argue that some of the strongest and most effective protections of children's interests are found in the self-regulatory collaboration of industry and the public.

We will also attempt, in the provision of the regulatory texts in the broadcast area, to expand on the background or context for their creation, the process of their realization, and the path of their evolution. In addition to helping to show why and how such regulatory texts came to be, that information may demonstrate why the goal of providing comparable protection for children in the virtual world may be challenging and elusive.

In the first part of this book, we will address television regulations, since television is still the medium with which children spend the most hours per week. We will review regulatory and self-regulatory measures – which mainly concern programming, sexual stereotypes, violence, and advertising – that various organizations have taken concerning shows for children. In the second part, we will describe regulations developed for film, videos, and video games intended for children, and will present a figure summarizing provincial regulations and classification systems. Finally, we will summarize existing measures that address children and the Internet in Canada, the European Union, the United Kingdom, the United States, and Australia. In the end, our goal is to provide specific answers to the question, "How are today's children protected in our new multi-screen environment?"

PART ONE

Television

The reality of publicly accessible broadcast television began in the United Kingdom in 1936, the United States in 1948, and Canada in 1952. However, since approximately 75 per cent of the Canadian population lives within about 200 kilometres of the Canada-US border, American commercial network television broadcasts began to bleed into Canada's principal urban centres starting in 1948. Although there were reportedly only 325 television sets in Canada in 1948, that figure grew exponentially by the time CBFT and CBLT began to broadcast in Montreal and Toronto in September 1952, and thereafter.

Television set penetration has been complete; in Canada in 2012 nearly every home (99 per cent) has a colour television. Moreover, two thirds of Canadian homes subscribe to cable, while close to one in four homes subscribe to satellite.[1] Furthermore, according to BBM Canada, every Canadian spends an average of more than twenty-six hours a week in front of a television screen.[2] Canadian children, defined in the Violence Code and the Broadcast Code for Advertising to Children as "persons under 12 years of age," watch television seventeen hours a week, while adolescents aged twelve to seventeen watch for a little over sixteen hours.[3]

In this book, we will draw a distinction between the regulations that apply to children and those that apply to the rest of the population. It is not our purpose to explain the socio-psychological background for the distinction but rather, accepting that reality, to describe the guidelines and regulations that define the presentation of television programs for children. While the CRTC establishes the rules and framework for other codified standards, broadcasting and advertising self-regulatory NGOs have created and administer many of the standards themselves. Such standards involve a broad range of broadcast content coverage.

In what follows, we describe the rules applicable to television programming and children developed by the principal stakeholders: the CRTC, the Canadian Association of Broadcasters (CAB), the Canadian Broadcast Standards Council (CBSC), the Canadian Broadcasting Corporation (CBC), Advertising Standards Canada (ASC, formerly the Canadian Advertising Foundation), the now-defunct Canadian Cable Television Association (CCTA), and the jointly created CAB-CCTA Action Group on Violence on Television (AGVOT), as well as provincial consumer protection agencies and Health Canada. While other organizations have intervened in various related consultative processes, few have had as direct an impact on the matters treated in this book; we will, however, note them where relevant.

1

The Canadian Radio-television and Telecommunications Commission

The Canadian Radio-television and Telecommunications Commission (CRTC) has existed since 1968, when it replaced the Board of Broadcast Governors.[1] A creature of parliament, the CRTC is an independent quasi-judicial regulatory agency. It regulates and supervises all aspects of the Canadian broadcasting and telecommunications systems.

The Broadcasting Act[2] gives the CRTC the mission to enforce the broadcasting policy it sets out in section 3, which defines the parameters of the Canadian broadcasting system. First, the act says that broadcasting is "a public service essential to the maintenance and enhancement of national identity and cultural sovereignty" and that radio frequencies are "public property."[3] While it is not germane to the purpose of this book, the issue of Canadian content (frequently referred to as "cancon") is worth noting here *en passant*. Section 5(2)(e) requires that broadcasters meet a Canadian content quota in order to favour the presentation of Canadian shows to Canadians. Almost all of the French- and English-language network licensing conditions thus stipulate that broadcasting must include specific percentages of Canadian programming.

Second, it recognizes that broadcasting in French and English, "while sharing common aspects, operate under different conditions and may have different requirements."[4] Third, it sets out the main objectives of the system as a whole. The system should, among other things, "through its programming and the employment opportunities arising out of its operations, serve the needs and interests, and reflect the circumstances and aspirations, of Canadian men, women and children, including equal rights, the linguistic duality and multicultural and multiracial nature of Canadian society, and the special place of aboriginal peoples within that society."[5] Fourth, the act assigns goals to broadcasting companies, as well as expectations concerning their programming. Finally, it mentions objectives related to the CBC, as the national public broadcaster, complementary television programming, and distribution undertakings.

In this way, the Broadcasting Act establishes that all of the components of the system must help to create and present Canadian programming, and lays out a series of specific principles that are central to the issues treated in this book:

> (g) the programming originated by broadcasting undertakings should be of high standard;
> (h) all persons who are licensed to carry on broadcasting undertakings have a responsibility for the programs they broadcast;
> (i) the programming provided by the Canadian broadcasting system should
>   (i) be varied and comprehensive, providing a balance of information, enlightenment and entertainment for men, women and children of all ages, interests and tastes,
>   (ii) be drawn from local, regional, national and international sources,
>   (iii) include educational and community programs, ...
> (j) educational programming, particularly where provided through the facilities of an independent educational authority, is an integral part of the Canadian broadcasting system.

In 1999, the CRTC decided not to intervene in the regulation of new media such as the Internet,[6] but in 2008, it held public hearings to re-examine the role of new media in the Canadian broadcasting system.[7] One of the commission's focuses was on whether or not there was a need to regulate Internet service providers. Until then, new media undertakings had enjoyed exemption orders and so had not been subject to any of the requirements of the Broadcasting Act. If the CRTC's conclusion had favoured the regulation of such services, its role would have likely expanded. However, in June 2009, the CRTC announced a new regulatory policy that maintained the status quo and continued to allow exemption orders to apply to new media undertakings (see part 4 for more detail). The commission stated that it would refer the legal issue of the applicability of the Broadcasting Act to Internet service providers to the Federal Court of Appeal.[8]

On 7 July 2010, the Federal Court of Appeal concluded that Internet service providers do not fall within the scope of the Broadcasting Act but rather the Telecommunications Act.[9] In February 2012, the Supreme Court of Canada reaffirmed that decision.[10] Although the CRTC regulates both Canadian telecommunications and broadcasting, in this book we will focus principally on broadcasting.

BROADCASTING RULES ESTABLISHED BY THE CRTC

In order to accomplish its mission, Parliament accords the CRTC a number of powers: it can adopt regulations governing the various categories of enterprises, and it can grant, renew, modify, or even revoke the licences of programming and program distribution companies. It can impose conditions of licence, investigate complaints, make orders, and, in limited circumstances not germane to the substance of this book, issue fines to ensure that companies comply with the Broadcasting Act.[11]

In 1987, the CRTC adopted new Television Broadcasting Regulations, replacing those of 1978. According to section 5 of the new regulations:

> 5 (1) A licensee shall not broadcast
> (a) anything in contravention of the law;
> (b) any abusive comment or abusive pictorial representation that, when taken in context, tends to or is likely to expose an individual or a group or class of individuals to hatred or contempt on the basis of race, national or ethnic origin, colour, religion, sex, sexual orientation, age or mental or physical disability;
> (c) any obscene or profane language or pictorial representation; or
> (d) any false or misleading news.

(1.1) For the purposes of paragraph (1)(b), sexual orientation does not include the orientation towards any sexual act or activity that would constitute an offence under the Criminal Code.

STANDARDS FOR PAY TELEVISION, PAY-PER-VIEW TELEVISION, AND VIDEO ON DEMAND

The pay television, pay-per-view (PPV) television, and video-on-demand (VOD) industry plays an increasingly important role in Canadians' lives. In 2009, these services generated profits of $3.1 billion – a 6 per cent increase over the $2.9 billion they earned in 2008. In comparison, the income of all other media plunged.[12] These services permit viewers to choose cinema and television programs from a broad selection, which makes adult content more readily accessible than it is on conventional television services. As a result, the CRTC requires, via conditions of licence, that these undertakings adhere to the Pay Television and Pay-per-View Programming Code regarding Violence and the Industry Code of Programming Standards and Practices Governing Pay, Pay-per-View and Video-on-Demand Services,[13] both of which are administered by the CBSC.[14]

The new Industry Code of Programming Standards and Practices lays down the principle that pay, PPV, and VOD services be "committed to the presentation of programming that is well balanced, of high quality, and of interest to a wide number of Canadians." The code acknowledges that such discretionary services "have more latitude to program material that is intended for mature audiences than is the case with conventional television services." As would be expected, program content must be consistent with all pertinent laws and regulations, and more amorphously, cannot be "offensive to general community standards." The code includes provisions relating to the rating and scheduling of such programming and the obligation to broadcast appropriate viewer advisories. It adds that pay, PPV, and VOD broadcasters must adhere to the Equitable Portrayal Code (a CAB code that was "created to ensure the equitable portrayal of all persons in television programming" in 2008 and is a condition of licence for all broadcasters), for which administrative responsibility lies with the CBSC.

2

The Regulation of Children's Programming

The Violence Code and the Broadcast Code for Advertising to Children define *children* as "persons under 12 years of age." *Adolescents* and *youth* are persons between the ages of twelve and seventeen.

THE CRTC'S ROLE

Although the 1991 Broadcasting Act does not explicitly touch on the issue of children's programming, over the years the CRTC has shown some interest in issues associated with the availability and quality of such programming. Since the CRTC has the power to regulate all aspects of Canadian television, it could, if children's programming became a matter of concern, regulate any broadcast-related matter that pertains to it. Apart from aspects associated with individual broadcast licences that we examine below, the commission participated in some general regulatory aspects of children's television programming in the early 1990s.

One such regulation relates to violence in television (which we address in depth in chapter 4). To illustrate the CRTC's role in this area: a petition to the prime minister brought by Quebec teenager Virginie Larivière in the fall of 1992 led to a series of events that resulted in the creation of a new broadcaster code dealing with television violence in October 1993.[1] The culmination of the deliberative codifying process was an (unusual) public event at which those who had participated in the drafting – including the CRTC, to which each draft and revision had been submitted along the way – were present. In the public notice accompanying that code, the CRTC emphasized the relationship of the new standards to children: "The Commission is generally satisfied that the CAB's revised Code achieves the appropriate balance between preserving freedom of expression and protecting the viewing public, especially children, from the harmful effects of television violence."[2] That primordial focus on children is reflected in article 2 of the code, which deals in detail with the issue of children and television and emphasizes the need for "particular caution in the depiction of violence" in children's programming, and elaborates on specific examples of the standards to be respected.

The CRTC also has regulations about television advertising directed at children, which we address in chapter 5. For instance, it established the Broadcast Code for Advertising to Children, which is administered by the children's advertising section of Advertising Standards Canada (ASC).[3] That code provides for pre-clearance of ads for children, as well as for the review of commercial messages about which members of the public have complained.[4]

MEANS OF INTERVENTION

Every broadcaster that wishes to use Canadian frequencies must apply to the CRTC for a licence.[5] The CRTC's authority to regulate broadcasting is complete. Section 9 of the Broadcasting Act describes its powers:

> 9 (1) Subject to this Part, the Commission may, in furtherance of its objects,
>
> (a) establish classes of licences;
>
> (b) issue licences for such terms not exceeding seven years and subject to such conditions related to the circumstances of the licensee
>
> (i) as the Commission deems appropriate for the implementation of the broadcasting policy set out in subsection 3(1), and
>
> (ii) in the case of licences issued to the Corporation, as the Commission deems consistent with the provision, through the Corporation, of the programming contemplated by paragraphs 3(1)(l) and (m);
>
> (c) amend any condition of a licence on application of the

licensee or, where five years have expired since the issuance or renewal of the licence, on the Commission's own motion;
(d) issue renewals of licences for such terms not exceeding seven years and subject to such conditions as comply with paragraph (b);
(e) suspend or revoke any licence;
(f) require any licensee to obtain the approval of the Commission before entering into any contract with a telecommunications common carrier for the distribution of programming directly to the public using the facilities of that common carrier;
(g) require any licensee who is authorized to carry on a distribution undertaking to give priority to the carriage of broadcasting; and
(h) require any licensee who is authorized to carry on a distribution undertaking to carry, on such terms and conditions as the Commission deems appropriate, programming services specified by the Commission.

The CRTC has several instruments to ensure that Canadian broadcasting reflects the Broadcasting Act's policy objectives. It is the fullest licensing authority and can mandate conditions of licence, its expectations, and the broadcaster's commitments, all of which apply to conventional and non-conventional broadcasters alike in the area of children's programming.

First, as all broadcasters and persons close to the television and radio industries know well, compliance with CRTC conditions of licence is mandatory. As we will discuss below, in addition to the many conditions attached to all broadcast licences, specialty channels for children and some educational channels have licences with conditions that specifically refer to children and young people.

Second, when the CRTC issues or renews a licence, it often notes its expectations in certain areas. While the commission expects broadcasters to respect such principles, it will not likely revoke a licence if they fail to fulfil them. In other words, CRTC expectations concerning children's programming are not the equivalent of conditions of licence.

Third, some broadcasters make specific commitments concerning children's programming when they apply for a licence. While these commitments are not considered conditions of licence, they are recorded in the application. It is, however, important to bear in mind that expectations and commitments can become conditions of licence at the time of future renewals, especially if the CRTC finds the broadcaster has exhibited a lack of respect for such commitments.

Finally, the CRTC can make mandatory orders that are enforceable like other federal or provincial superior court orders.

In order to show how the CRTC intervenes and to draw a picture of television in Canada today, we will now take a closer look at television networks with licences that contain specific conditions, expectations, and commitments relating to children's programming.

CONVENTIONAL CHANNELS

Conventional channels fall into two categories: public and private. Until 1999, CRTC renewals of private conventional channel licences included specific requirements for children's programming. For example, in 1992, TVA's licence renewal contained the following expectation: "The Commission expects Télé-Métropole to revise its programming policy as it pertains to Canadian children's programming, particularly in light of the need for programs of this type that reflect the concerns and aspirations of young 'Québécois.' The Commission expects the licensee to present Canadian programs for children on a regular basis."[6] Similarly, in 1994, CTV's licence renewal contained the following condition: "In each year of the licence term, CTV [must] broadcast in network sales time a minimum of one hour per week of regularly scheduled Canadian programming directed to children. The Commission expects the licensee, in adhering to this condition, to give strong emphasis to the presentation of new, original programs of the highest possible quality."[7]

When the CRTC reviewed Canadian television policy in 1999, it concluded that there were enough shows for children in network programming and that it was not necessary to impose any further requirements in this regard. In a public notice, it stated:

> The majority of conventional English- and French-language television broadcasters offer children's programming on a regular basis, and the system as a whole provides a wide variety of Cana-

> dian and foreign programming directed to children and youth. In addition, children's programs have an extended life cycle, as "evergreen" programming enjoyed by many generations. The recognition of the excellence of Canadian children's programs, and its exportability ensure its availability without a regulatory requirement.[8]

In other words, the CRTC decided it was not necessary to require that all broadcasters air a minimum percentage of children's programming, as it does for Canadian content. This decision not to subject broadcasters as a group to a regulatory framework for children's programming does not mean, however, that the CRTC will refrain from imposing children's programming requirements in individual broadcaster licences as a function of each broadcaster's mandate. For example, at a 2001 licence renewal, CTV agreed to broadcast a minimum of 2.5 hours of children's programming per week. This was consistent with the CRTC's view that it would be reasonable to expect CTV to provide programs that meet the needs of all age groups, including children.

The CBC and its French-language counterpart, Société Radio-Canada (SRC), have special licences. Section 3 of the Broadcasting Act defines the CBC and SRC as national public broadcasters, which means it is Parliament that specifies their operating procedures and policies. For example, Parliament requires that the CBC and SRC devote a certain number of hours a week to programs for young people. Their mandate reflects this programming commitment, as it refers to the provision of quality educational and entertainment programming for children and youth.

When the CRTC renewed SRC's licence in 2000, it emphasized the network's special role, which is to reflect the values of all of Canada in its programming. The CRTC also expressed certain expectations of the commitments that SRC needed to make with respect to children's programming, namely, to air twenty hours a week of such programming, if not more. The CRTC went so far as to add a specific condition of licence in its decision: "In each year of the licence term, the licensee shall broadcast an average of at least 4 hours per broadcast week of original Canadian programming directed to children under 12 years of age."[9] In its rationale, the CRTC expressed its wish to "ensure that the

CBC will continue to broadcast an adequate number of original programs [as] children's programs, by definition, have a long life and lend themselves well to repeat broadcasts."[10] It emphasized that, "especially in a small market like French Canada, it is important for the public broadcaster to contribute to the development and broadcast of new programs that reflect the new generation." At the same licence renewal, SRC committed to broadcasting 75 per cent Canadian content throughout the day, and 80 per cent Canadian content during prime time (from 7:00 to 11:00 p.m.).

In the CBC's case, the CRTC has formulated an expectation rather than a condition of licence concerning children's programming, in the following terms: "In each year of the new licence term, the CBC will broadcast a minimum of 15 hours per week of Canadian programs directed to children 2 through 11 years of age, and 5 hours per week of programs directed to youth (ages 12–17)."[11] This expectation was established because of the CBC's responsibility, as a public broadcaster, to provide shows for nearly all Canadians and to offer children and young people informative, educational, entertaining programming. The CRTC requires the CBC, as a condition of licence, "to report on the implementation of these commitments in its Annual Report."

EDUCATIONAL CHANNELS

The CRTC defines educational television as a "service that offers educational programming and whose operation is the responsibility of an educational authority."[12] Five Canadian provinces have educational broadcasters: Alberta has ACCESS: The Education Station, which has been privatized since 2005 and is now operated by CTVglobemedia; Quebec has Télé-Québec; Ontario has TVOntario (TVO) and its French-language counterpart, TFO; British Columbia has Knowledge Network; and Saskatchewan had the Saskatchewan Communications Network (SCN), which Rogers Broadcasting Limited acquired from Bluepoint Investments Inc in June 2012).[13] The CRTC has established specific conditions of licence that relate to children's programming for three of these networks; namely, ACCESS, Télé-Québec, and TFO.

ACCESS, which has a mandate to present programs that inform, educate, and enlighten, must devote at least 60 per cent of the broadcast year to "educational programming with clear learning objectives ... or educational programming directed to pre-school children."[14]

Télé-Québec made a number of commitments concerning programming for children when its licence was renewed in 2009. First, it indicated that its choice of programming was established along three major lines, one of which was programming for young people. In support of this position, Télé-Québec pointed out that, in each year of its previous licensing period, it had broadcast thirty-five to sixty-five hours of children's programs per week, which was well beyond its commitment of twenty-one hours. It reiterated its twenty-one-hour weekly commitment, and also committed to broadcasting new programs and, increasingly, an Internet presence appropriate for each age group. When the CRTC renewed Télé-Québec's licence, it added a condition of licence requiring the broadcaster to "caption 100% of its programming over the broadcast day," in compliance with its policy on closed captioning.[15]

TFO has a mission to foster French in Ontario and, to that end, it devotes a large part of its programming to young people. When its licence was renewed in 2008, TFO acknowledged that French-speaking children and youth in Ontario need to see themselves in, and identify with, the programs they watch. Thus, the CRTC expected TFO to broadcast at least thirty-nine hours a week of Canadian shows for children and youth aged two to seventeen during its new licence period, though it did not make it a condition of licence.[16]

While TVO, Knowledge Network, and SCN have licences free of conditions relating to children's programming, they each broadcast a large number of shows for that audience and have made certain commitments. The CRTC expects TVO to broadcast forty hours of educational children's content every week, Knowledge Network to broadcast fifty-four hours of shows for children and youth, and, SCN to devote 40 per cent of its broadcasting to children's programs.[17]

SPECIALTY CHANNELS FOR CHILDREN

Private specialty television channels often have unique conditions of licence that relate to their mandates, and specialty channels for children must make commitments that meet specific criteria. During hearings on licence renewals, the CRTC consistently reviews and assesses whether a broadcaster fulfilled its conditions of licence, expectations, and commitments during the previous licence period.

The CRTC defines a specialty service as a "service that offers a specific type of programming aimed at a specific audience group."[18] In Canada, there are a number of specialty television channels with programming intended partly, or wholly, for children. Depending on their mandates, the CRTC has laid down rules that such channels must comply with to ensure their children's programming is of high quality. In fact, the CRTC licences these specialty services on the basis of their mandates, which differentiate them from one another and operate like conditions of licence.

Networks with a mandate and programming designed partly or entirely for children include Aboriginal Peoples Television Network (APTN), Teletoon (in English, and Télétoon in French), BBC Kids, Nickelodeon Canada (formerly Discovery Kids), Family Channel, YTV, Vrak.TV, Treehouse TV, and, more recently, Vrak Junior and Yoopa (TVA Junior).

APTN's mandate is to serve Canadian Aboriginal audiences in French, English, and several Aboriginal languages. While neither this objective nor CRTC regulations concern programming for youth, the network nonetheless states its commitment to broadcast series for children. Moreover, APTN is subject to a condition of licence that requires it to devote at least 75 per cent of the broadcasting year to Canadian shows.[19]

Télétoon (French) and Teletoon (English) have a specialty cartoon broadcasting mandate. While cartoons and animated programming are not necessarily *children's* programming, many animated shows do target young audiences, and Télétoon and Teletoon each broadcast around one hundred hours of programming for young people weekly. Surprisingly, the CRTC does not have any expectations or conditions regarding the content of this programming, though it does align with the CRTC's objectives since 3 million children in Canada aged two to eleven watch it. Furthermore, since at least 60 per cent of the broadcasting day on these channels must be devoted to Canadian content, young people benefit from the CRTC's attention to it. Moreover, these channels have to spend 47 per cent of their income on acquiring Canadian shows and ensure that 75 per cent of their Canadian programming comes from independent producers. Finally, Télétoon and Teletoon have to deliver 700 half hours of new Canadian productions in English and French during their licence period.[20]

BBC Kids obtained its licence in 2000 with a mandate to offer educational, entertaining, high-quality programming for children and youth aged two to seventeen. The CRTC imposed quotas as conditions of licence on BBC Kids: 65 per cent of its programs must be for children aged two to eleven, and the majority of that percentage must target children aged six to eleven, with the remaining 35 per cent of programs targeting youth aged twelve to seventeen. Moreover, no more than 15 per cent of the network's weekly content may be from the United States.[21]

Discovery Kids also obtained its licence in 2000, with a mandate to provide English-language programs for children of all ages. The CRTC required that the channel ensure children would find its programs "a fun, entertaining way to satisfy their natural curiosity with stimulating, imaginative programming that asks the questions of how? and why? and awakens the power of the mind. The schedule shall include interactive programming as well as action-packed programs with unforgetable [*sic*] characters and real life young heroes."[22]

The CRTC considers BBC Kids and Discovery Kids to be category 2 services. This means they do not compete directly with other networks and have more accommodating, flexible conditions of licence. However, to avoid competition among Canadian services, the CRTC requires that they devote no more than 25 per cent (BBC Kids) or 10 per cent (Discovery Kids) of their broadcasting to dramas and comedies. Moreover, each channel had to reserve at least 35 per cent of its broadcast year for Canadian shows.

In September 2008, the CRTC granted Corus Entertainment, which was also the owner of Discovery Kids, a licence to launch the YTV OneWorld channel on the following conditions: "The licensee shall provide a national, English-language Category 2 specialty programming service offering programming from around the world targeting children aged 6 to 17 and their families. The schedule will include programs devoted to entertainment, humour, travel, games and science and technology."[23] On 2 November 2009, Corus replaced Discovery Kids with Nickelodeon Canada, which took its place using the licence that had been issued to YTV OneWorld.

Family Channel's conditions of licence provide that its shows have to be aimed exclusively at children and young people aged seventeen and under and their families. Consequently, the channel must comply with the following conditions: it may not broadcast any shows that are classified as adult or restricted, that reflect any Ontario Film Review Board equivalent of those classifications, or that belong to the categories of news, religion, education, or sports. The channel has to dedicate at least 25 per cent of its total broadcast time and 30 per cent of its prime time hours (between 6:00 p.m. and 10:00 p.m.) to Canadian shows.[24]

YTV, which has a broad mandate to offer national programming of English-language specialty shows for children, youth, and their families, also faces broadcasting quotas. Each year, the channel must devote at least 30 per cent of its shows to children aged five and under and at least 48 per cent of its shows to young people aged six to seventeen. At most, 22 per cent should target families. Like on other networks for children, music videos must not account for more than 5 per cent of YTV's shows. In both 2006 and 2009, the CRTC rejected YTV's request to change these percentages to focus more on children aged six to seventeen, as it found that the channel is still a major source of content for children aged five and under. The CRTC also requires that YTV "devote 100% of the programs in the drama category distributed in the evening broadcast period to programs of particular interest to children, youth and their families through the use of a protagonist that is developed with children, youth or families in mind, examples of which would include an animated character, super hero, animal, child or youth." YTV must allot at least 60 per cent of its broadcast year and 60 per cent of the evening broadcast period to Canadian programs, and expend 40 per cent of its annual revenue on acquiring and investing in Canadian programming. YTV must also broadcast ninety hours a year of "original, first-run Canadian programs."[25]

Vrak.TV is a French-language channel with a mandate to offer nationwide specialty programming for French-speaking children and youth up to age seventeen. At a 2006 licence renewal hearing, Vrak.TV applied to add the fifteen-to-seventeen age group to its mandate, which concerned some interveners as the channel is the only French-language specialty service that targets children of all ages. The CRTC, however, saw benefits to the extension of the age group: "With this greater flexibility, the licensee will be able to meet the needs of adolescents aged 15 to 17 years, an age group that is not widely served by broadcasters."[26] At the same time, the commission took care to ensure that "this additional flexibility should not be to the detriment of programs targeted to groups aged 0 to 5 years, 6 to 11 years, or those aged 12 to 14 years." It did not do this by the imposition of a condition of licence but instead by expressing its expectation that Vrak.TV will "continue to establish its program schedule in a manner that reflects, in an equitable fashion, all of the age groups that it serves in compliance with its nature of service." In addition, the channel has to devote no less than 60 per cent of the shows that it broadcasts during the day and 50 per cent of the evening broadcast period to Canadian content. It also has to provide 104 hours a year of original first-run Canadian French-language productions and invest at least 41 per cent of its annual income on Canadian programming rights, development, and promotion expenditures.[27]

Treehouse TV's first condition of licence is that all programs broadcast between 6:00 a.m. and 9:00 p.m. must target children aged six and under. This channel is the only one that targets such a young English-speaking audience, and the CRTC seeks to ensure that no show meant for an audience other than that made up of pre-school children will be broadcast on Treehouse TV. The condition of licence also requires that no more than 5 per cent of programming aired after 9:00 p.m. be in the form of music video clips and other music and dance shows, since that type of broadcasting targets an audience other than preschoolers. Treehouse TV must also broadcast a high percentage of Canadian shows, which much compose at least 70 per cent of its content during the day, and at least 60 per cent in the evening. Moreover, it has to spend 32 per cent of its income on the acquisition of or investment in Canadian programs, and the CRTC noted its commitment to provide 325 half hours of original Canadian productions during its seven-year licence period.[28]

In March 2006, the CRTC issued Astral Media an operating licence for its Vrak Junior channel. One of its conditions of licence stipulated: "The licensee shall provide a national, French-language Category 2 specialty programming service that offers programming dedicated to children aged two to six years, except between 9:00 p.m. and midnight, when the schedule may include programs of interest to parents of pre-school children."[29] After a few years, though, Astral Media abandoned its plan to launch Vrak Junior and created Playhouse Disney Télé, which began to broadcast in July 2010 and now broadcasts as Disney Junior.

In June 2009, TVA Group applied to the CRTC for a licence to operate the TVA Junior channel. In its application, it argued that young French speakers in Canada are poorly served and that a French-language specialty channel devoted to children aged two to six, similar to the Treehouse service for English-speaking children, would resolve the problem. Consequently, in February 2010 the CRTC issued a licence to TVA Junior on the condition that it provide a national category 2 specialty broadcasting service in French exclusively targeted to children aged two to six.[30] Before the channel launched, Astral Media argued that Videotron (a cable distribution company that belongs to Quebecor, the owner of Groupe TVA) had refused to distribute Vrak Junior in order to avoid competition with TVA Junior. Videotron denied this, and TVA Junior launched on 1 April 2010 under the name Yoopa.

SELF-REGULATION

While broadcasters must comply with the commitments they make when they receive or renew a licence, the CRTC has not, since the creation of the new Violence Code in 1993, had any involvement in issues related to the content of children's programming on television. Instead, complaints about such programming, or indeed about children-related issues with family or adult broadcast content on private television stations, networks, or services, are dealt with by the effective self-regulatory Canadian Broadcast Standards Council (CBSC).[31]

Pierre Trudel, a professor in the Centre for Research in Public Law at the Université de Montréal's faculty of law, defines self-regulation as "recourse to voluntary norms developed and accepted by those engaging in an activity."[32] When it operates effectively in the direction of desired public policy, self-regulation simplifies the public regulatory process in any sphere of professional or commercial activity. To do this, it takes full advantage of the motivation that exists within any industry to deal with its own dirty laundry at home.

Like the analogous bodies that exist in other professions, Canadian broadcasters believed they could respond to any complaints or concerns from members of the public without outside intervention. Consequently, the private broadcasters, through the CAB, developed norms that have the informal (or occasionally formal) approval of the CRTC. While they do not technically have the force of law, such norms have been sufficiently supported by the CRTC that even those that are not conditions of licence have come to be virtually equivalent to those that are.

THE CBSC

In February 1988, the Canadian Association of Broadcasters (CAB) produced the CAB Code of Ethics in which broadcasters acknowledged the need to comply with standards of professional integrity in their relations with advertisers and agencies.[33] For instance, though the CBSC has not rendered any decisions based on it, clause 4 of the code enunciates the following principles relating to children's programs:

> 1 Recognizing that programs designed specifically for children reach impressionable minds and influence social attitudes and aptitudes, it shall be the responsibility of broadcasters to provide the closest possible supervision in the selection and control of material, characterizations and plot.
> 2 Nothing in the foregoing shall mean that the vigour and vitality common to children's imaginations and love of adventure should be removed. It does mean that such programs should be based upon sound social concepts and presented with a superior degree of craftsmanship, and that these programs should reflect the moral and ethical standards of contemporary Canadian society and encourage pro-social behaviour and attitudes. Broadcasters should encourage parents to select from the richness of broadcasting fare the best programs to be brought to the attention of their children.[34]

The CBSC enforces compliance with the Code of Ethics. Founded by the CAB in 1990, the CBSC acts as an interlocutor between the public and broadcasters.[35] It is responsible for the application of the codified standards and the adjudication of complaints about potential breaches of those norms.[36] In addition, the CBSC has, as one of its objectives, the duty to inform the public of the existence of those standards, which it does in no small measure via its website. Its most public face is undeniably the recourse it provides to members of the public for concerns they may have about broadcast content; when complainants are not satisfied by the initial dialogue phase of the process, the CBSC formally resolves their complaints.[37] Moreover, it does so without the formality of Canadian government regulatory sanctions, much less the extraordinarily heavy-handed American regulatory penalties.

CBSC decisions are rendered by one of its seven panels, of which two are national and five regional. The national panels – one of which deals with conventional television and the other with specialty services – render decisions concerning nationally broadcast programming from specialty services or networks, that is, if "complaints regarding the program have arisen in three or more Regions."[38] The regional panels deal with complaints about broadcasters in their respective regions. There are five panels, one for each of the Atlantic region, Quebec, Ontario, the Prairies, and British Columbia. The adjudicating panels sit as seven-person national panels or six-person regional panels, made up in each case of adjudicators who represent the public and the industry. The goal in every instance is to have equal representation from both sectors but, if there is ever an imbalance due to adjudicator availability issues, no panel can sit with more representatives of industry than of the public.

THE CBSC DECISION BASE

The more than five hundred decisions the CBSC has rendered since 1991 (all of which are posted on its website) have established the common law determining the acceptability or not of the substance of broadcast content. The CBSC's jurisprudence has defined the standards, and although a complainant dissatisfied with a decision can ask for the CRTC to review the complaint, the CRTC has never reversed a CBSC decision.[39] Moreover, on several occasions – even in the case of decisions that involve public broadcasters, which do not fall under the jurisdiction of the CBSC – the federal regulator has cited principles established by the CBSC in its own decisions.

A VOLUNTARY PROCESS?

To conclude our observations associated with the self-regulatory component of the regulatory process, we will address the voluntary versus obligatory nature of the CBSC structure. The only voluntary aspect of the system is the choice to be or not to be a member of the council. As of the moment of the writing of this book, just over 750 licensees, that is to say, all significant broadcast groups in the country have chosen to be members of the CBSC, and are therefore subject to its jurisdiction.[40] All CBSC members are obliged to respect the standards in any codes that apply to them.[41] There is nothing voluntary about that adherence. Moreover, the Violence Code and the Equitable Portrayal Code are CRTC-imposed conditions of licence for all television broadcasters, public as well as private, whether or not they are members of the CBSC.

There are a number of CRTC expectations concerning programming for children. These include sensitivity to the importance of the availability and quality of children's programs, and the fulfilment of commitments to abide by the codes that deal especially with the depiction of violence and equitable portrayal in children's programs and advertising directed to children. These expectations are self-applied, if not exactly self-regulatory, because they are guidelines for the channels rather than legal obligations; however, they can become conditions of licence with consequences.

In short, since 1999, the CRTC has imposed specific, particular conditions on individual channels but has avoided setting general conditions for children's programming. It uses operating licences in an efficient manner and takes advantage of self-regulation to manage the Canadian broadcasting industry. In the next chapters of this book, we will show how industry codes developed from self-regulation formally regulate some aspects of television programs for children, such as stereotypes, violence, and advertising.

3

The History of the Regulation of Stereotypes and Equitable Portrayal

The CRTC has touched on the issue of stereotypes in programming since its creation but, until the creation of the Equitable Portrayal Code in 2008, had never taken any concrete regulatory steps on the broad issue of ethno-cultural stereotyping. It had, however, taken steps in the area of gender stereotyping that played an important role in the evolution of the regulatory approach that ultimately led to the creation of the Equitable Portrayal Code. Having tools to deal with stereotypes is all the more important in regulating children's television, as exposure to recurring stereotypes on television is most likely to affect young minds. Here then is a brief history of the progression towards the Equitable Portrayal Code.

MEASURES TAKEN BY THE CRTC

In the early days of the dialogue about the potential deleterious effects of stereotypes on radio and television, much of the focus was directed towards the treatment of women in and by media. It was only more recently that the focus shifted to ethnicity, race, and culture as well as gender. In 1979, the federal government published *Towards Equality for Women*, a national action plan intended to promote the equality of women in Canadian society and eliminate discrimination based on gender.[1] In response, the CRTC formed a task force to develop guidelines and policy recommendations to ensure a more positive and realistic portrayal of women in broadcast media.

Given its mandate to develop guidelines to promote the elimination of sexual stereotypes on radio and television, the task force chose to focus on stereotypes of women. Its report, *Images of Women: Report of the Task Force on Sex-Role Stereotyping in the Broadcast Media*, published by the CRTC in 1982, contained a number of recommendations that the CRTC later implemented by requesting that broadcasters submit reports on initiatives taken to limit the occurrence of sex-role stereotyping in their programs. Broadcasters' and advertisers' associations also developed self-regulatory measures in this respect.[2]

In 1986, the CRTC assessed the progress that had been made in the area of gender portrayal in broadcasting since 1979. In a public notice entitled Policy on Sex-Role Stereotyping in the Broadcast Media,[3] it noted that three objectives determined its approach: (1) reduction of the occurrence of sex-role stereotypes; (2) commitments to change on the part of broadcasters and advertisers; and (3) raised awareness among stakeholders.[4] It reported on the work that had been done and made recommendations so that industry would continue its efforts. In that same policy statement, the CRTC announced its intention to require all broadcasters, whether or not they were members of the Canadian Association of Broadcasters (CAB), to comply with the CAB's Voluntary Guidelines on Sex-Role Stereotyping:

> The Commission notifies all its radio and television broadcasting licensees, both CAB and non-CAB members, that it intends to impose a condition of licence when their applications for licence renewal are considered, requiring their adherence to the CAB self-regulatory guidelines, as amended from time to time and accepted by the Commission. As noted earlier, these guidelines are presently being revised by the CAB and, when accepted by the Commission, will henceforth be referred to as "The Broadcasting Industry's Self-Regulatory Code on Sex-Role Stereotyping."[5]

The CRTC asked the CAB to take additional, more concrete steps, which led to the 1990 publication of the Sex-Role Portrayal Code for Television and Radio Programming,[6] which became a condition of licence imposed on all radio and television licence holders that produce forty-two or more hours of programs per week, and on radio and television channels that distribute seven or more hours of network shows per week.[7] The code was administered by the CBSC from the council's creation and was approved by CRTC in 1991.[8] It remained in force until the Equitable Portrayal Code, which includes protections for the portrayal of gender along with race, national or ethnic origin, colour, religion, age, sexual orientation, marital status, or physical or mental disability, replaced it in 2008.

THE CBC'S PROGRAM POLICIES CONCERNING STEREOTYPES

In 1979, the CBC added provisions to its program policies in which it made a commitment to reflect the role of women in Canadian society and developed language guidelines to fight sexism. This policy has been revised a number of times since 1979. The latest version, Stereotypes in CBC/Radio-Canada Programming, came into effect in 2005 and includes directives that apply to all types of programs, including those intended for children.[9] The CBC's policy uses the *Webster's Dictionary* definition of the notion of stereotype, which reads as follows: "A fixed or conventional notion or conception as of a person, group, idea, etc. held by a number of people and allowing for no individuality, critical judgment, etc."[10]

In its policies, the CBC acknowledges the dangers of broadcasting programs that convey stereotypes, and tolerates certain such programs on the condition that the stereotypes they contain are essential components.[11]

THE CANADIAN ADVERTISING FOUNDATION'S GENDER PORTRAYAL GUIDELINES

Advertising Standards Canada (ASC; formerly, from 1982 to 1997, the Canadian Advertising Foundation, or CAF, and, for nearly two decades before that, the Canadian Advertising Advisory Board, or CAAB) administers the advertising industry's self-regulatory program. The ASC responds to complaints from the public concerning advertising in all media, including broadcast. Although the CBSC has authority to deal with broadcast advertising under clauses 13 and 14 of the CAB Code of Ethics, as a matter of practice, it only deals with complaints about broadcast advertising that it receives from the public and that fall squarely within the ability of the broadcaster to influence, such as the scheduling of commercials. Where the substance of the complaint relates to content, such as gender portrayal, the CBSC forwards it to the ASC for resolution.

In 1981, the CAAB set up guidelines dealing with sex-role stereotyping and an Advisory Committee on Sex-Role Stereotyping, which was responsible for "an on-going information and 'sensitizing' program with industry associations and groups" and encouraging the public to send the committee "complaints about advertising which they feel is not in accord with the Guidelines." The original guidelines, entitled Gender Portrayal Guidelines, were significantly revised in 1993 and apply to all Canadian paid media. The most recent version of the document contains norms on several important topics: authority, decision-making, sexuality, violence, diversity, and language.[12] These guidelines concern advertising aired by Canadian broadcasters, whether produced in Canada or abroad. The original advisory committee was replaced in 1993 by advisory panels on gender portrayal, which were themselves superseded a number of years ago by ASC's consumer response councils, which are invited to consider the principles of the gender guidelines when adjudicating complaints about related issues.

THE VARIOUS CAB CODES

While the CAB was engaged with other industry groups in the development of sex-role portrayal standards, it was also working to update its forty-five-year old Code of Ethics. The 1988 wholesale revision of that code included a new clause 3, which addressed sex-role stereotyping: "Recognizing that stereotyping images can and do have a negative effect, it shall be the responsibility of broadcasters to exhibit, to the best of their ability, a conscious sensitivity to the problems related to sex-role stereotyping, by refraining from exploitation and by the reflection of the intellectual and emotional equality of both sexes in programming."[13]

In 1990, as noted above, the CAB published its Sex-Role Portrayal Code for Television and Radio Programming, which became a condition of licence for all broadcasters and was administered by the CBSC. The code's general principles and guidelines applied to all programs broadcast on television (or radio). They therefore had to be taken into account in the production of children's programming. One of the general principles was written specifically with children in mind: "Broadcasters shall be sensitive to the sex role models provided to children by television and radio programming. In this context, programmers shall make every effort to continue to eliminate negative sex role portrayals, thereby encouraging the further development of positive and progressive sex role models. The 'sexualization' of children in programming is not acceptable, unless in the context of a dramatic or information program dealing with the issue."[14] Another guideline that concerns children, entitled "Exploitation" under clause 4, reads as follows: "Television and radio programming shall refrain from the exploitation of women, men and children. Negative or degrading comments on the role and nature of women, men or children in society shall be avoided. Modes of dress, camera focus on areas of the body and similar modes of portrayal should not be degrading to either sex. The sexualization of children through dress or behaviour is not acceptable."[15] Finally, the general principles and guidelines stated in the code also apply to advertising (for a discussion of advertising, see chapter 5).

In 1999, the CRTC created a public notice that dealt with the broad television policy framework.[16] In the document, the CRTC noted gender portrayal but not broad diversity issues in its discussion of societal issues, though it strongly endorsed cultural diversity: "The Commission will expect all conventional television licensees (at licensing or licence renewal) to make specific commitments to initiatives designed to ensure that they contribute to a system that more accurately reflects the presence of cultural and racial minorities and Aboriginal peoples in the communities they serve. Licensees are expected to ensure that the on-screen portrayal of all minority groups is accurate, fair and non-stereotypical."[17] The CRTC also noted the distinction between reflection of cultural diversity in programming and portrayal, and added an important caveat: "Without accurate and sensitive portrayal, programming runs the risk of stereotypical representation."[18]

Then, in August 2001, the CRTC called on the CAB to create and fund an industry and community task force to address the reflection and portrayal of Canada's cultural diversity on television.[19] The resulting Task Force for Cultural Diversity on Television, comprised of five industry representatives and four non-industry representatives, was formed in July 2002. The task force's mission was two-fold: first, to study how cultural diversity is portrayed on Canadian television; and second, to develop recommended best practices and industry initiatives for broadcasters. The task force published its conclusions in July 2004 in a report entitled *Reflecting Canadians – Best Practices for Cultural Diversity in Private Television*. One of the recommendations was that the CAB examine its industry codes to ensure that they were compatible with the task force's conclusions. In September 2005, another report, commissioned by the CAB and titled *The Presence, Portrayal and Participation of Persons with Disabilities in Television Programming*, followed.[20] That report noted that the broadcasting industry lacks sufficient standards and points of reference with respect to people with disabilities, and recommended assessing existing codes to remedy this lack.

The next step was for the CAB to replace its outdated and narrowly purposed Sex-Role Portrayal Code with a new code, the title of which reflected its much broader coverage and purpose. The Equitable Portrayal Code was announced on 17 March 2008, and was "created to ensure the equitable portrayal of all persons in television and radio programming."[21] In its opening words, Canada's private broadcasters declare their recognition of "the cumulative societal effect of negative portrayal and, by creating this Equitable Portrayal Code, [they] establish common standards to prevent such portrayal." They do this in two ways: first, by extending the coverage of the previous code from gender to all identifiable groups on the basis of "race, national or ethnic origin, colour, religion, age, gender, sexual orientation, marital status or physical or mental disability"; and second, by extending the Sex-Role Portrayal Code's limited protections against exploitation, degradation, and inequality to all forms of negative portrayal, including stereotyping, stigmatization, victimization, derision of myths, traditions, or practices, degrading material, and exploitation.

The general principles of the Equitable Portrayal Code are consistent with and complement the Radio Television Digital News Association Code of (Journalistic) Ethics and the ASC's Canadian Code of Advertising Standards. Like the other broadcaster codes, the Equitable Portrayal Code is administered by the CBSC, which deals with complaints and renders decisions related to those codified standards.[22]

It would not be an exaggeration to observe that the standards applicable to the requirements for equitable portrayal and related prohibitions of negative portrayal based on matters of race, national or ethnic origin, colour, religion, age, gender, sexual orientation, marital status, or physical or mental disability are as thorough in their coverage as any that exist in any jurisdiction. To the extent that those rules are reflected in television broadcasters' programming practices, they inevitably inure to the benefit of children, as well as adult members of the viewing audience.

4

The History of the Regulation of Violence in Media

In the 1970s, the Canadian public began to express growing concerns in regards to the depiction of violence on television. In response to this burgeoning Canadian discomfort, in 1975 the Ontario government announced a Royal Commission on Violence in the Communications Industry, which was followed within months by a CRTC Symposium on Television Violence that called for specialists to study the issue of television violence. One of the results of these initiatives was a collective awareness of the complexity of the problem and the need for further research. In 1977, the *Report of the Royal Commission on Violence in the Communications Industry* confirmed the reality and the magnitude of the problem. It concluded that there was a link between violence in media and the level of violent crime in society, but it was unwilling, or perhaps unable, to quantify the strength of the link. The report discussed its original goals and its conclusion in the following terms:

> The Commission was to determine if there is any connection or a cause-and-effect relationship between this phenomenon and the incidence of violent crime in society. The short answer is yes. How serious an effect is less clear ... If the amount of depicted violence that exists in the North American intellectual environment could be expressed in terms of a potentially dangerous food or drink additive, an air or water pollutant such as lead or asbestos or mercury, or other hazard to humans, there is little doubt that society long since would have demanded a stop to it, as society has done in denouncing hazards that are directly measurable in terms of physical illness or death.[1]

In response to its fourth instruction, namely, to make recommendations, the royal commission noted that the popularity of American television programs with Canadian audiences made regulation complicated: "The constantly increasing flow of television violence on US networks and Canadian private networks and private stations goes on at all hours, including times when children are watching."[2] The commission framed its conclusion in this respect as follows: "We find that Canadians generally are watching more and more US-made television with much higher levels of violence than that produced here or anywhere else."[3] Prior to the release of that report, no regulations existed in Canada, voluntary or otherwise, to control violence on television.

BACKGROUND

Several historical events fuelled the acceleration of the regulatory direction in the area of violence in media.

The first was an event that is still commemorated annually on a broad scale in Canada more than two decades after its occurrence. In 1989, an acknowledged misogynist killed fourteen women at Montreal's École Polytechnique. The resulting societal response was an outcry for government action of various kinds to prevent future violent occurrences, among other things, by curtailing television violence, presumed by some to contribute to such events. In 1990, the minister of communications asked the chair of the CRTC to examine possible links between violence on television and violence in society.

Then, in 1992, eleven-year-old Marie-Ève Larivière was kidnapped, raped, and murdered.[4] Her thirteen-year-old sister, Virginie Larivière, convinced that there was a link between television violence and her sister's death, circulated a national petition that called for the adoption of a law against television violence. She aimed to collect one million signatures and approached Prime Minister Brian Mulroney to be one of them, a request to which he of course agreed. Ultimately, she collected 1.5 million signatures and Mulroney sent her petition to the House of Commons Standing Committee on Communications and Culture for consideration. Virtually overnight, Virginie Larivière alerted the national consciousness to the issue of television violence and made it a focus of collective concern. Keith Spicer, the then-chair of the CRTC, characterized the young teenager's role: "Virginie became the Joan of Arc of TV violence – an innocent, unassailable, uncompromising heroine."[5]

The regulatory snowball began its inexorable roll downhill, gathering both snow and momentum. No one was prepared to slow down its progress.

THE CRTC'S INVOLVEMENT

In 1992, the CRTC launched a program designed to control violence on television.[6] The long-term objective of the program was to render violence on television socially unacceptable. The CRTC began by commissioning and publishing two studies. The first, entitled *Summary and Analysis of Various Studies on Violence and Television*, provided an overview of how other countries dealt with the conundrum of violence on television.[7] The second, entitled *Scientific Knowledge about Television Violence*, summarized some 200 scientific studies on television violence and its effects.[8]

Following publication of these reports, the CRTC prompted members of the broadcasting industry to fight against violence and establish a dialogue among themselves. The commission required broadcasters to develop voluntary measures and cable companies to design their own anti-violence strategy. It requested that the leaders of the Canadian pay television industry and specialty services discuss the issue of violence with broadcasters and cable companies. It also held meetings with other stakeholders (including the Canadian Teachers' Federation, the Canadian Home & School and Parent-Teacher Federation, the CAF, the CBC, and various Canadian producers) to discuss ways of collaborating to eliminate violence on television.

THE FORMATION OF THE ACTION GROUP ON VIOLENCE ON TELEVISION

In 1993, a pivotal conference on television violence was held with the support of the CRTC at the C.M. Hincks Institute in Toronto. During the conference Minister of Communications Perrin Beatty proposed a five-point strategy: (1) adoption of a very strict code of ethics concerning drama and music videos; (2) development of an awareness campaign; (3) promotion of a competition among the principal Canadian advertisers with the goal of encouraging them not to buy time slots during programs with violent scenes; (4) collaboration with the United States to solve this issue; and (5) creation of the Virginie Larivière Television Award to honour those who have contributed to reducing television violence and producing quality youth programs. The participants also discussed the importance of developing Canadians' ability to critically evaluate media, or what has come to be known as media literacy.

In February 1993, following the Hincks Conference, the Action Group on Violence on Television (AGVOT) was created. The two principal co-founders were the Canadian Association of Broadcasters (CAB) and the Canadian Cable Television Association (CCTA), but other television industry stakeholders of the 1990s participated, including the CBC, the Canadian Film and Television Production Association (CFTPA), Association des producteurs de films et de télévision du Québec (APFTQ), the Association of Canadian Advertisers (ACA), the Alliance for Children and Television (ACT), and pay TV, specialty program, and pay-per-view companies. CRTC and Department of Canadian Heritage representatives attended AGVOT meetings as observers.

In accordance with the CRTC's desire for broadcasters to develop voluntary measures to reduce violence in media and determine acceptable conditions for its broadcast, AGVOT produced a four-point program, which the CRTC summarized as follows:

> Self-regulation by the industry, closely monitored by the CRTC;
> A national program classification system;
> New technology that would give viewers, especially parents, direct control over which programs enter their homes;
> Public awareness and media literacy programs.[9]

Next, AGVOT adopted a general statement of principles concerning the broadcast of television violence. In the statement, AGVOT established the basic structural standards that would govern the presentation of violent content in television programs. The most important guidelines in the statement, as summarized by the CRTC, are:

> Programs that contain gratuitous violence will not be shown on television.
>
> The Canadian broadcasting industry commits to uphold freedom of expression and to maintain journalistic, creative and programming independence and integrity.
>
> All licensed broadcasters accept the responsibility for the programs they broadcast, and are committed to act effectively and expeditiously in resolving programming concerns expressed by their viewers.
>
> Each licensee will prepare program schedules giving due consideration to the nature of the service and the expected viewing audience. Each licensee also recognizes its special responsibility when selecting programs directed at children.
>
> In order to facilitate informed viewing choices, licensees will provide their viewers with appropriate information on the content of their programs consistent with the nature of the service.
>
> Each member of the Canadian broadcasting industry undertakes to adopt a code dealing with violence in television programming, based on this General Statement of Principles.[10]

AGVOT members agreed to adhere to the principles of this general statement and to design action plans to reduce television violence.[11]

THE INDUSTRY'S SELF-REGULATORY INITIATIVES

The Canadian Association of Broadcasters Violence Code

The CAB Violence Code was a precursor to the Hincks Conference and the formation of AGVOT and its general principles.[12] Originally created in 1987, by the 1990s it was widely recognized as insufficiently compulsory to effectively regulate televised violence. Pursuant to the above initiatives, the private broadcasters prepared drafts of new codified standards, which were circulated among the interested parties, sent to the CRTC for comment and reaction, and finally announced at a major press conference in October 1993. The Voluntary Code regarding Violence in Television Programming came into effect as of 1 January 1994.[13] From that date on it was imposed on all television broadcasters as a condition of licence upon the issuance of new licences or the renewal of existing ones. (By way of exception, however, the commission announced that it would be prepared, on application, to suspend this condition of licence for broadcasters in good standing with the CBSC.) The one section of the code that was anticipated in it but was unavailable as of that date was a program classification system outlined in article 4, an important informative component but not so essential that it was worth delaying the other content and scheduling standards that were ready to serve the public interest as of 28 October 1993.

The code's statement of principle, which reflected the post-Hincks AGVOT principles noted above, reads as follows:

> 1.1 Canadian private broadcasters understand and accept they have a responsibility to their viewers, in addressing the issue of violence on television.
> 1.2 By their adherence to this Code of practice, Canadian private broadcasters are publicly endorsing the following principles:
> 1.2.1 that programming containing gratuitous violence not be telecast,
> 1.2.2 that young children not be exposed to programming which is unsuitable for them,
> 1.2.3 that viewers be informed about the content of programming they choose to watch. ...
> 1.5 The depiction of violence within children's programming shall not be so realistic as to threaten young children, to invite imitation, or to trivialize the effects of violent acts.
> 1.6 The portrayal of violence within drama programming shall be relevant to the development of character, or to the advancement of the theme or plot.
> 1.7 Within news and public affairs programming, the depiction of violence shall be relevant to the nature of the event or story being reported.[14]

Reflecting the statement of principle, the first article of the code deals with a basic program content issue; namely, gratuitous or glamorized violence:

> 1.1 Canadian broadcasters shall not air programming which:
> • contains gratuitous violence in any form;[15]
> • sanctions, promotes or glamorizes violence.

Another critical component of the statement of principle focuses on the suitability of programming for children under age twelve, and so the code also contains specific rules concerning such programs. They are so central to the theme and purpose of this book that they appear here in full:

> 2.1 As provided below, programming for children requires particular caution in the depiction of violence; very little violence, either physical, verbal or emotional shall be portrayed in children's programming.
> 2.2 In children's programming portrayed by real-life characters, violence shall only be portrayed when it is essential to the development of character and plot.
> 2.3 Animated programming for children, while accepted as a stylized form of storytelling which can contain non-realistic violence, shall not have violence as its central theme, and shall not invite dangerous imitation.
> 2.4 Programming for children shall deal carefully with themes which could threaten their sense of security, when portraying, for example; domestic conflict, the death of parents or close relatives, or the death or injury of their pets, street crime or the use of drugs.
> 2.5 Programming for children shall deal carefully with themes which could invite children to imitate acts which they see on screen, such as the use of plastic bags as toys, use of matches, the use of dangerous household products as playthings, or dangerous physical acts such as climbing apartment balconies or rooftops.
> 2.6 Programming for children shall not contain realistic scenes of violence which create the impression that violence is the preferred way, or the only method to resolve conflict between individuals.
> 2.7 Programming for children shall not contain realistic scenes of violence which minimize or gloss over the effects of violent acts. Any realistic depictions of violence shall portray, in human terms, the consequences of that violence to its victims and its perpetrators.
> 2.8 Programming for children shall not contain frightening or otherwise excessive special effects not required by the storyline.

Once again reflecting the statement of principle, this time in relation to the issue of children's access to programming that may not be suitable for them, the code includes rules related to program scheduling. One such rule involves the *watershed*, the time between 9:00 p.m. and 6:00 a.m. in which programming intended exclusively for adult audiences can be broadcast. The watershed has played an important ongoing role in television scheduling. The wording of the relevant codified standard is as follows:

> 3.1 Programming
>
> 3.1.1 Programming which contains scenes of violence intended for adult audiences shall not be telecast before the late evening viewing period, defined as 9 pm to 6 am.
>
> 3.1.2 Accepting that there are older children watching television after 9 pm, broadcasters shall adhere to the provisions of article 5.1 below (viewer advisories), enabling parents to make an informed decision as to the suitability of the programming for their family members. ...
>
> 3.2 Promotional material which contains scenes of violence intended for adult audiences shall not be telecast before 9 pm.
>
> 3.3 Advertisements which contain scenes of violence intended for adult audiences, such as those for theatrically presented feature films, shall not be telecast before 9 pm.

The code also anticipates the value of information to parents, indeed to all consumers, in making choices of suitable television content for their homes. Accordingly, it includes directives on the need for viewer advisories, which also have special safeguards regarding children, even though it is not expected that young persons will be the principal individuals who exercise viewing choices:

> 5.1 To assist consumers in making their viewing choices, broadcasters shall provide a viewer advisory at the beginning of, and during the first hour of programming telecast in late evening hours which contains scenes of violence intended for adult audiences.
>
> 5.2 Broadcasters shall provide a viewer advisory at the beginning of, and during programming telecast outside of late evening

hours, which contains scenes of violence not suitable for children.

Finally, the code includes rules regarding the broadcast of programming that includes violence against women and specific groups:

> 7.2 Broadcasters shall ensure that women are not depicted as victims of violence unless the violence is integral to the story being told. Broadcasters shall be particularly sensitive not to perpetuate the link between women in a sexual context and women as victims of violence. ...
> 8.1 Broadcasters shall not telecast programming which sanctions, promotes or glamorizes violence based on race, national or ethnic origin, colour, religion, gender, sexual orientation, age, or mental or physical disability.

The CBSC's Implementation of the Violence Code

The CBSC administers the Violence Code. It did so for the very first time on 24 October 1994, in regards to what was then the most commercially successful children's television program of all time: *Mighty Morphin Power Rangers*. The resulting decision became one of the CBSC's most highly publicized.[16] The series, which was broadcast by Global Television Network, YTV, Fox Network, and CFTM-TV and its sister stations in the Réseau TVA), was a crucial test for the CBSC because of some scepticism about how the new code would be applied: as heavily as it appeared to be written, or daintily?

Although more than fifty complaints were made directly or indirectly to the CBSC, only two (dated 29 April and 2 May 1994) remained to be adjudicated after the other complainants appeared to be satisfied by the broadcaster's explanation of what it had broadcast and why. Although the series ran on other non-CBSC member stations or services, the two complaints, which both came from Ontario viewers, concerned only Global. After receiving notification of the complaints from the CBSC, Global responded by arguing that *Power Rangers* was no different from other children's shows. That explanatory letter read in part: "*Mighty Morphin Power Rangers* is perhaps one of the most popular children's programs currently being broadcast. In fact, during one personal appearance event in Los Angeles, more than 35,000 children and parents came to see the stars of the show ... Since the dawn of television, children's programming, including most cartoons, have depicted 'good' triumphing over 'evil.' *Mighty Morphin Power Rangers* continues this long-standing tradition."[17] Given the nature of the complaints and the expectation that standards breaches (if any) would be found to be repetitive, the CBSC supplied its Ontario panel with the logger tapes of all ten episodes broadcast during the two weeks corresponding to the dates of the complaints. The panel's conclusions were unanimous. The adjudicators found that all of the episodes broadcast by Global "were essentially identical, structurally speaking" and – though they conceded that the show's producers and therefore broadcaster had seriously attempted to convey didactic and moral messages – all violated several of the standards of the Violence Code.

First, the panel found that *Power Rangers* violated article 2.1, which requires that there be very little violence in children's programming. Of the dramatic content of each episode, the panel found that 25 to 35 per cent consisted of fight sequences, which was in its view clearly in excess of "very little violence," although that standard has never been quantified. The panel stated: "While the Council understood clearly that each program attempted to convey a didactic or moral message to its viewers, whether relating to family values, the need for pollution control and recycling, or other matters, it was the view of the Council that these valuable messages were overwhelmed by the quantity of violence surrounding their transmittal. Far from containing very little violence, the series appeared to convey considerable violent physical activity."[18]

Second, noting the codifiers' distinction between real-life and animated characters, the CBSC found that the series contravened article 2.2, which stipulates that, where real people play the roles, violence should only be used if it is essential to plot and character development. The panel pointed out: "Defining a plot in terms of violence [or the character development of the protagonists as fighters] does not constitute satisfaction of the requirement that the violence is permissible when essential to the development of that plot."

Third, the panel noted that the show violated article 2.6, which proscribes programming for children that creates the impression that violence is the preferred, much less only, way to resolve conflict. It pointed out: "None of the episodes so much as offered an alternative to the conflict resolution central to each plot other than the application of one fighting technique or another ... Not once in any of the episodes was there depicted any attempt to resolve conflict by any technique other than fighting."

Fourth, the panel found the show's absence of blood or other evidence of injury problematic, though some commentators at the time, including Global, misunderstood the finding or considered it counter-intuitive. Although the Global representative stated: "*Power Rangers* does not feature death, blood or dismemberment in any of the episodes," they missed the essential point that the consequences of violence should not be minimalized or hidden. According to article 2.7 of the Violence Code: "Any realistic depictions of violence shall portray, in human terms, the consequences of that violence to its victims and perpetrators." As the panel explained: "Those who view this absence of physical damage as a positive rather than a negative consideration lose sight of the importance to children of understanding the consequences of their acts. In real life, punching and kicking do have physical results in almost every instance."

Finally, flowing to some extent from its failure to respect article 2.7, the panel found that *Power Rangers* contravened article 2.5 because of the risk it could encourage children to imitate what they saw on television. As the panel pointed out: "The absence of consequences led to the additional Council concern regarding the encouragement of imitation by children of what they see the Power Rangers doing. Suggesting that the martial arts kicking and punching techniques do not have serious, or even minor, physical consequences invites, if not encourages, the seemingly risk-free imitation of the physical acts of aggression by children who have not reached the age of discernment, namely, the very audience for this program."

To its credit, Global spent a not-inconsiderable sum in an effort to edit the remaining episodes of the season to comply with the CBSC's decision.[19] In the end, the broadcaster stopped airing the series a few months later. Although the CBSC had not received complaints about the French-language version of the series, Télé-Métropole removed it from its programming immediately. So did YTV, which ceased broadcasting the show the day after the release of the CBSC decision despite the fact that it was not then a member of the CBSC and so not legally subject to the ruling.[20]

The decision did not resolve every concern; indeed, a burdensome problem was anticipated by the panel despite its conclusions. The series was, after all, still available via broadcasters[21] not subject to the authority of the CBSC, and could still reach the very audiences the code was designed to benefit, namely, Canadian children and families. The concern was expressed in the following way:

> In rendering this decision, though, the Council is troubled. While it is entirely comfortable with the substance of its conclusions, it deplores the fact that there are no corresponding requirements for adherence to these principles on the part of YTV or the cable carriers of Fox Network programming. The Council's view of *Mighty Morphin Power Rangers* is a function of non-compliance with a set of principles established with the collaboration of the CRTC for the benefit of all Canadians. The issue is the message, not the medium by which it is being delivered.

The fact that signals from American broadcasters were not subject to regulation by either the CRTC or the CBSC raised two issues. On the one hand, was it possible to protect Canadian children from the effects of inappropriate content carried on a specific channel if they could see the same content on other channels? On the other hand, was there a way to ensure that no Canadian broadcaster that complied with the Violence Code would be at a competitive disadvantage "vis-à-vis ... a *foreign*-originating signal accessible to everyone with basic cable service"? The CBSC's uneasiness that some television broadcasters were not governed by a system similar to its own put pressure on the CRTC to establish a regulatory system to apply to all channels available in Canada (which we will discuss below).

In 2002, a complaint similar to those from 1994 was made concerning a new Power Rangers series, *Power Rangers Wild Force*, broadcast by CTV. The complainant argued that the series was in no way different from the original *Mighty Morphin Power Rangers* that had created controversy eight years earlier. According to him, both series shared a similar name, as well as the same concept, target audience, and production company. On top of it all, the quantity of violence in

Wild Force seemed to the complainant to be the same as in *Mighty Morphin Power Rangers*.

The CBSC disagreed. After the National Conventional Television Panel analyzed the complaint and the relevant episodes, it concluded that *Power Rangers Wild Force* did not violate the provisions of the Violence Code because, in general terms, it "reflect[ed] the producers' remedying of almost all of the concerns of the Ontario Regional Panel in 1994."[22] More specifically, the panel concluded that: (1) "the level of fighting or violence had dropped by 50% or more from the 1994 series"; (2) "considerably more effort was made to define the individual Power Rangers characters by dramatic indicators of personal traits and to make the fighting sequences relevant to the plots" in the new series; (3) there was "almost no fighting that the Panel considers realistic in nature," which meant that there was no issue regarding the use of violence to resolve conflict; and (4) almost none of the violence in the new series, whether realistic or fantastical, was shown without consequences, as "limping, injured, bandaged Rangers are the regular result of fighting sequences."

In short, the CBSC concluded that Canadian broadcasters had scrupulously respected the lessons of the creation of the Violence Code and its interpretation in 1994. No program targeting children has been the subject of complaints to the CBSC since that time.

The Action Plan of the Canadian Cable Television Association

Towards the end of 1992, the CCTA presented the Community Channel Leadership Project focussed on television violence. The project, which brought together cable television programming employees and people living in the regions in question, aimed to establish measures to improve the public's media awareness.

In 1993, the CCTA formed a task force with a mandate to study American programs broadcast by cable and to present its findings to the CRTC. In parallel, the CCTA began to develop a code and action plan on television violence. It submitted that proposed code and action plan, entitled *Violence on Television – Action Plan* to the commission on behalf of the cable industry in the fall of 1994. The code had not yet been accepted by the commission as of April 1995. At the violence hearings in October 1995, the CCTA presented a document to the television violence hearings[23] in which it advocated the following actions:

- the establishment of a classification system that will provide viewers with information on program content;
- the deployment of technology that will work in concert with the classification system to allow viewers to screen out programming they do not with to receive, and
- a collaborative industry-wide information campaign to assist viewers on how to make informed viewing choices.[24]

These measures reflected the position of the cable television industry, which opposed the institution of regulations that rest on the principle of cable companies' intervention in rebroadcast content and third-party control of individuals' television program choices – measures that were proposed in the CRTC document that was the basis for the then upcoming violence hearings.[25] The CCTA pursued this approach in order to promote development and subscriber use of control technology. The cable television industry was aware that, as long as such technology was not available, the CRTC might choose to establish means to counter the problem of reception of programs from abroad containing violent scenes, as it proposed in the appendix to the Notice of Public Hearing of 3 April 1995. Wishing to avoid any CRTC proposal that might entail any obligation on cable companies to curtail their signals, during the transition period the CCTA was ready to substitute programming from American services under the following conditions:

- the programming is a series and is found to be too violent for children based on a full public review, by the CRTC,[26] of the programming in question;
- the CRTC has established a minimum number of people that would have to complain about a given program in order to trigger a review by the CRTC;[27]
- the programming is aired before the 9:00 p.m. watershed hour; and
- cable companies are explicitly required by CRTC regulation to

provide substitute programming and the decision is widely publicized.

The CCTA also proposed that, as soon as a cable company had installed subscriber-control technology, it would be free of any obligation to comply with the above conditions. In the end, with the timely arrival of V-chip, or anti-violence chip, technology, it never became necessary to implement the program-substitution proposal.

Moreover, in 1993, the industry had decided to apply the Sex-Role Portrayal Code for Television and Radio Programming and the Violence Code to programs produced by cable television companies for community channels. These measures were not the equivalent of altering or curtailing signals distributed, but not produced, by cable companies. In the end, subscriber-controlled technology in the form of the V-chip resolved the issue and although the CCTA, disbanded in February 2006, did not remain around long enough to benefit for more than a decade from the fruits of that development, the cable companies and satellite broadcast distribution undertakings have done so. All cable television companies save the largest have since turned towards the Canadian Cable Systems Alliance (CCSA), which represents independent cable television companies.

Individual Cable Company Initiatives

Two cable television companies – Videotron and Shaw – demonstrated an early interest in curbing television violence and took measures to do so.

In the fall of 1994, Montreal-based Videotron set up a parental control system on Videoway, the table-top converter it had first introduced for subscribers in 1989. The system allowed users to block access to a channel or selection on the Videoway menu at all times.[28] Vidéotron developed the system in response to concerns expressed by the public about violence and other perceived adult subjects such as nudity, sexual content, and coarse language. By using the system, parents could prevent their children from watching any programs and channels they considered inappropriate. Videoway was discontinued in 2006.

In 1995, Edmonton-based Shaw Communications Inc tested the V-chip along with Superchannel in the Edmonton area. Rogers and CF Cable TV also joined Shaw in those early trials.[29]

The Pay Television and Pay-per-View Programming Code regarding Violence

Pay television and pay-per-view television licensees worked together to develop The Pay Television and Pay-per-View Programming Code regarding Violence, which the CRTC approved with a few amendments in 1994.[30] Pay television and pay-per-view licensees have been subject to its provisions since 1 January 1995, and the CRTC requires compliance with the code as a condition of licence for these companies. The code deals exclusively with violence, including violence in programming for children, and has rules similar to those in the CAB Violence Code. Moreover, as in the case of the CAB's code, the pay television and pay-per-view television code provides that no program containing violent scenes intended for an adult audience shall be shown other than during the watershed.

The code also has provisions concerning program classification. Pay television and pay-per-view television licensees must comply with the rating assigned by their home province's film classification body. If a program has not been rated, licensees must assign a rating in accordance with the criteria developed by the classification body of the province where the program originated. Article 4.6 states: "Viewer advisories and ratings will appear 'on-air' in both written and spoken forms, in all programming not suitable for children."

With respect to advertising material, pay television and pay-per-view television licensees are subject to the provisions of the CAB Violence Code. In the case of pay television, where the service provides content previews, a special rule is provided in article 5, which reads in full: "Where programming is aired during preview periods Licensees will exhibit only programming that meets the same standards of scheduling and content contained in the Canadian Association of Broadcasters Violence Code. This same provision will apply to any promotional material provided to cable operators, for distribution on barker channels. Any clips so provided which are unsuitable for children will be clearly identified as unsuitable for broadcast before 9:00 p.m. or after 6:00 a.m."

In addition to the steps taken to develop a shared code, other pay and pay-per-view television stakeholders adopted measures intended to raise viewers' awareness of television violence. For example, in 1993, Astral Media (then Communications Astral) announced its intention to insert advisories when it broadcast films. It began to project a flashing white "V" on a red square at the beginning of, and every thirty minutes during, all films containing violent scenes. Various pay television channels also announced their intention to refrain from broadcasting programs containing scenes of violence. Some specialty programming companies, such as Vision TV, MuchMusic, and MusiquePlus, drafted statements of intent aimed at reducing the presentation of violent programs on television. Specialty services also submitted a code on violence to the CRTC.

As the market for televisual entertainment grew, many companies sought to mount new, unique specialty channels. In 1995, the CRTC adopted a policy on the distribution of video game programming following a request from Sega to offer subscribers a video-game service. Cable companies and video-game service enterprises are thus authorized to provide video-game programming under certain conditions. Some of the conditions were established in response to concerns about violence, stereotypes, advertising, and children:

- The undertaking's programming complies with the Canadian Association of Broadcasters' Sex-Role Portrayal Code for Television and Radio Programming, Violence Code and Broadcast Code for Advertising to Children, as amended from time to time and approved by the Commission.
- The video games offered via the undertaking's programming service are categorized and information is provided to subscribers indicating, at a minimum, the suitability of individual games for use by children and adolescents.[31]

Moreover, the CRTC invited all other enterprises planning such services to provide a protection mechanism such as that suggested by Sega. The mechanism would use an integrated V-chip in the channel adaptor that would enable parents to use a password to limit access to games they considered inappropriate for their children.

The CBC's Program Policy Concerning Violence

While private broadcasters led the self-regulatory agenda on television violence, the national public broadcaster, the CBC, was a participant in AGVOT and has always been sensitive to viewer concerns about violence. Indeed, in the 1980s it adopted a program policy with respect to violent programs, the most recent version of which, entitled Violence in Programming and Violence in Children's Programming, dates from 1994.

Generally, the policy provides that children should not be exposed to adult program content as, understandably, some children react very badly to the presentation of television programs containing scenes of aggression and violence. For this reason, emphasis is on spotlighting inspiring, exemplary role models and on encouraging peaceful dispute resolution and cooperation. The following are examples of television content that the CBC cites as possibly harmful if presented in children's programs:

- Excessive aggression, including torture and sadistic beatings;
- Undue cruelty shown by adults to children, or children to other children;
- Criminal actions that children can easily imitate, such as hanging scenes, etc.;
- Cartoon material that attempts humour through stripping people of their dignity, through the portrayal of aggression linked with sexual overtones or with stereotypes.[32]

As a television broadcaster, the CBC is subject to all the requirements of the CAB Violence Code and also, therefore, respects its scheduling, classification, and viewer advisory rules.

HOW PLANNED NATIONAL REGULATION BECAME CONCRETE

The CRTC's Objectives

Faced with all the industry's self-regulatory efforts, the CRTC had to take substantial action to knit all the various approaches into a single cloth.

In 1993, the House of Commons Standing Committee on Culture and Communications held hearings on television violence in order to gauge the scale of the phenomenon. A few months later, it published a report entitled *Television Violence: Fraying Our Social Fabric*, in which it made twenty-seven recommendations that required the participation of all stakeholders. Among other things, it endorsed the CRTC's voluntary cooperation approach to the Canadian and American industries.

A document entitled *Canada and TV Violence: Cooperation and Consensus* discussed measures taken with respect to violence on television, and summarized the five guiding principles underlying the CRTC's approach, as follows:

1 abandon an ideological, legalistic, and therefore combative approach in favour of a cooperative strategy recognizing TV violence as a major mental health problem for children;
2 adopt the goal of protecting children, not censoring adults, in order to strike a balance between the right to freedom of expression and the right to a healthy childhood;
3 stick to a focused agenda on gratuitous or glamorized violence, not diffusing efforts by adding on sex, foul language, family values, specific feminist concerns, or other distinct, more controversial issues;
4 bring all players to the table – broadcasters, advertisers, producers, parents, teachers, psychiatrists, and the regulator;
5 have both a short-term and a long-term perspective.

The CRTC's four specific objectives expressed in the document were to:

- Establish veritable industry-wide codes of conduct;
- Better inform viewers through a program rating system;
- Strengthen viewers' discretionary power using the anti-violence chip, in other words, the V-chip;[33]
- Change attitudes through public information and media awareness programs.

After the controversy surrounding the CBSC's *Mighty Morphin Power Rangers* decision, and, in particular, the CBSC's challenge regarding the public's easy access to problematic channels by merely clicking different numbers on their remote control, the CRTC held regional consultations on television violence in the fall of 1995, followed by a national public hearing in October. The consultations provided the public, the industry, and the CBSC with an opportunity to comment on the approach that should be taken to television violence. In the resulting Policy on Violence in Television Programming, the CRTC stated its intention to develop program rating classification systems and announced an acceptable blocking technology that would function in tandem with that system.[34]

In March 1996, in a report entitled *Respecting Children: A Canadian Approach to Helping Families Deal with Television Violence*, the CRTC outlined its policy with respect to television violence. It stated that the adoption of industry codes and a rating system would provide 10 per cent of the solution to the problem of violence on television, while V-chip technology would provide another 10 per cent. Finally, public awareness and media literacy programs would account for 80 per cent of the solution. The salient points of the CRTC's policy were as follows:

- As of September 1996, licensees of programming undertakings would be responsible for encoding a rating for violence in the programs they broadcast, using a system that is compatible with V-chip technology.
- As of September 1996, distribution undertakings will be responsible for making affordable V-chip devices available to subscribers.
- The commission designates AGVOT to develop an acceptable rating system. The rating system that is used should be informative and readily understandable to the viewer, and should consist of four to six levels. The development of such a system should involve input from the public, programmers and distributors, and must be submitted to the Commission for approval prior to the September 1996 implementation date.
- If AGVOT does not have a satisfactory V-chip decodable classification system approved by that date, the commission will expect the licensees of programming undertakings to classify programs according to the system employed in the second and current rounds of V-chip trials.
- Licensees of cable and other distribution undertakings will also be responsible for ensuring that, as of September 1996, and not later

than January 1997, programming on non-Canadian services distributed on their systems is encoded with a meaningful, parent-friendly rating for violence that may be read by the V-chip technology.

- If American programming is not encoded at its point of origin with a rating system acceptable to the commission, distribution undertakings will be responsible for developing and implementing alternative methods for ensuring that the programming on the US television signals they distribute is encoded with ratings for violence.
- The commission will expect the industry to conduct marketing and information campaigns to ensure that subscribers are aware of the availability of V-chip devices, how to obtain them, and how to use them.
- The commission notes that pay television and pay-per-view services should continue to use the ratings of the provincial rating boards for the feature films they broadcast. Similarly, the commission notes that, given the familiarity with, and acceptance of, the Régie du cinéma's rating system in Quebec, French-language broadcasters in that province should use that system. The commission encourages the industry to work toward integrating the rating schemes of the provincial rating boards, including the Régie, into a single system that can be used by all programming undertakings.
- The commission expects to be informed as to whether the CBSC, will act as a clearinghouse for the exchange of ratings information.[35]
- The commission encourages licensees, when producing or scheduling programming directed to children, to choose high-quality, non-violent programs.[36]

Through this policy, the CRTC required broadcasters and cable companies to develop a rating system compatible with the V-chip within the prescribed time frame. The CRTC also took a position on programs imported from the United States and stated that American broadcasters must rate the programs they air in Canada or Canadian cable broadcasters would do so, using a V-chip compatible system.

National Implementation of a Classification System and the V-chip

In 1993, AGVOT had begun to assess film and video rating systems that could be used in English Canada. (The Quebec broadcasting industry had chosen to retain the rating system already in use, which had been developed by Quebec's Régie du cinéma.)[37] In 1994, AGVOT conducted a survey to learn about the opinions of English-speaking Canadians on a new, shared rating system. The findings showed that Canadians favoured the creation of a joint rating system that would include advisories about violence, nudity, adult themes, and offensive language. Generally, respondents said that young people under the age of sixteen should not be exposed to violent or mature content or to foul language.[38] Following the survey, AGVOT continued to develop a rating system. Though its members had different interests and offered different programming services, they managed to agree on the following general principles:

- The primary purpose of any classification system should be to help Canadian parents make informed choices about programs for and with their children.
- Any rating system used by the broadcasting industry must be created with this intention. It will have to take into account the specific television viewers targeted by the programming and reflect the requirements of the various applicable broadcasting industry codes.
- The integration of this rating system with other rating systems, such as those used for films and home video rental, is not appropriate for all broadcasting services.

All of the stakeholders were aware that policies such as AGVOT's rating system would only be effective if an agreement was signed with the primary audiovisual content providers, that is, the American television and film industry. While achieving this had seemed unlikely a few years earlier, US Congress had recently made decisions that indicated there was the possibility of collaboration in order to establish a North American rating system.

One such decision was to adopt the Telecommunications Act of 1996, which includes the following provisions:

> Sec. 551(c) Requirement for manufacture of televisions that block programs – Section 303 (47 U.S.C. 303), as amended by subsection (a), is further amended by adding at the end the following:
>
> (x) Require in the case of an apparatus designed to receive television signals that are shipped in interstate commerce or manufactured in the United States and that have a picture screen 13 inches or greater in size (measured diagonally), that such apparatus be equipped with a feature designed to enable viewers to block display of all programs with a common rating, except as otherwise permitted by regulations pursuant to section 330(c)(4).[39]

The Federal Communications Commission (FCC), the American regulatory body with authority over communications, was then (and remains) responsible for establishing both the rules to implement these legislative provisions and the date on which they would come into effect. The legislation also provided that program distributors had one year to voluntarily develop codes for programs with violent, sexual, or indecent content, and to broadcast signals that matched the ratings. Otherwise, a committee would be created to develop guidelines instead. The industry expressed its intention to institute a voluntary television program classification system before 1 January 1997.

Finally, the American broadcasting industry and the cable television industry commissioned a number of studies, including the National Television Violence Study on violent scenes shown on American television, which was published in February 1996.[40]

At the CRTC's request, Canadian broadcasting, cable, and production companies met as AGVOT in 1996 to complete a Canadian rating classification system. Though the CRTC's request was limited to a system that targeted violent content, AGVOT quickly saw that program classification could not be restricted to violence. It correctly observed: "A system which focused only on violence would not adequately serve the needs of viewers. There could be programs that contained no violence, yet still not be suitable for younger audiences due to other types of content such as language, nudity, sexuality and/or mature themes."[41] The findings from the 1994 AGVOT consultations confirmed that the rating classification system had to take all such adult-oriented content into consideration. Thus, a system was developed that would include all of these types of content, giving television viewers information about programs beyond what the CRTC required.

The resulting system assigns children's programs, dramas, reality shows, and feature films different ratings.[42] The rating refers in effect to an evaluation of content according to specific, standardized guidelines that reflect generally accepted stages in child development. Some programs, such as news, sports, documentaries, talk and variety shows, and music videos are exempt from classification. Foreign programs are also assigned a Canadian rating when they are aired by Canadian broadcasters.

In concrete terms, the rating appears in the form of an icon in the upper left-hand corner of the screen at the beginning of the program for a period of no less than fifteen seconds. The icon indicates what age group the program targets in terms of the quantity and nature of the violence, offensive language, sex, and mature themes it contains.[43] The rating system also contains V-chip-compatible information.

The V-chip is a device integrated into analog televisions that makes it possible to electronically encode program classifications according to the rating assigned by broadcasters. The V-chip detects electronic information in the programming, which enables the device to block certain programs in accordance with the user's choices.

The rating system and the V-chip are tools that enable parents to choose what kinds of content their children can see, but they are, needless to say, not a replacement for parental supervision. Moreover, some parents will have greater (or lesser) sensitivity or tolerance for certain kinds of content and will choose different levels of content restriction depending on their own views. There is no one-size-fits-all approach to classification, viewer advisories, and the watershed. These are all tools provided by broadcasters to help parents make the choices appropriate to their own homes. All in all, the CRTC describes the set of broadcaster-provided controls as follows:

- prevent the showing of gratuitous or glamorized scenes of violence on TV
- declare a 9 p.m. cut-off time for showing violent scenes. Programs aired before 9 p.m. can't show violent scenes that are intended for adult audiences

- establish rules for children's programs that limit and control any depictions of violence
- establish rules for scenes of violence that appear on news and public affairs programs
- require written advisories and announcements at the beginning of any program that may contain violent scenes, as well as similar advisories throughout the program.[44]

While the deadline for making the V-chip and rating classification system available in Canada was originally September 1996, the CRTC later granted an extension until the beginning of the fall 1997 television season.[45]

In 1997, AGVOT tested the V-chip across Canada to ensure that the findings of the tests begun by Shaw in 1994 rang true under real conditions. This also made it possible for parents, public interest groups, and those specializing in children's use of media to assess the system. AGVOT presented its planned rating classification system on 30 April 1997, and the CRTC approved it on 18 June. Since the CRTC realized that broadcasters could not all use the same rating system because of differences in the kinds of networks as well as the language of broadcast, it allowed different rating systems to be employed across Canada:

- English and third-language conventional and specialty broadcasters use AGVOT's classification system
- French-language broadcasters use the classification system of the Régie du cinéma du Québec, which is Québec's provincial film board
- Pay, pay-per-view and video-on-demand services use the classification system of the provincial film board in their home province
- American stations that are directly available in Canada use the United States TV Parental Guidelines; other foreign stations directly available in Canada use their home countries' rating systems, where such systems exist.[46]

Though there had been progress, it was clear to the CRTC that the fall 1997 deadline could not be met. V-chip technology was still not perfect and there were uncertainties in the United States, and both factors militated against getting the mechanism on the market as quickly as was desired. In order to provide some information and benefit to the public in the meantime, broadcasters agreed to air classification icons at the beginning of the fall season anyway.

The problems with the V-chip came, on the one hand, from the many different rating systems that made it more complicated to finalize the technology and, on the other hand, from the fact that large-scale manufacturing of the mechanisms could not begin until the United States adopted the technology. Since the ratings system approved by the FCC would determine which technology would be offered to American consumers, and since that dominant market would clearly drive the V-chip agenda in both the United States and Canada, the mechanism's arrival to market was unavoidably delayed. Finally, the FCC required implementation of V-chip technology in July 1999 so that new television sets would be equipped with it starting in January 2000.

The classification system came into effect in September 1997, when Canadian broadcasters began to air the ratings icons. By 2001, most analog television sets larger than thirteen inches on the Canadian market had V-chips.[47] By March 2001, all Canadian broadcasters coded rating information in accordance with the V-chip, and by 2005 the chip and the ratings classification system were well established. Full responsibilities for the administrative duties concerning these two mechanisms were transferred to the CBSC on 1 March 2007.

The CBSC became the self-regulatory organization that administers the codes concerning violence and equitable portrayal in broadcasting. It is now responsible for everything related to the rating classification system and V-chip, and it has reported that between 2000 and February 2008 the number of complaints concerning television violence dropped by around 22 per cent.[48]

Other Stakeholders

Finally, a number of associations and groups intervene regularly on the issue of violence and the role of media in young people's lives, especially concerning television and video games. Though this list is not exhaustive in any way, these associations include the Canadian Paediatric Society, the Canadian Teachers Association, the Canadian

Home and School Federation, and the Ontario Violence in the Media Coalition. The latter represents a range of sectors, including parents, teacher federations, and student associations, that are committed to work to overcome the influence of media violence on young people. Other groups include Positive Alternatives for Children Everywhere (PEACE, also known as Travail de réflexion pour des ondes pacifiques, or TROP), a non-profit, Quebec-based organization, and Edupax, which specializes in violence prevention, peace education, and media literacy. Finally, Parents Matter (parentsmatter.ca), an excellent website sponsored by the Canadian Association of Family Resources Programs, features a long list of parenting sites that deal directly or indirectly with a variety of issues, some including media and violence.

5

The History of the Regulation of Advertising

INTRODUCTION AND CONSTITUTIONAL ISSUES RELATED TO QUEBEC'S CHILDREN'S ADVERTISING REGULATION

Advertising plays an important, influential part in the world of television. Indeed, it constitutes an undeniably formative influence in the minds of those who receive its messaging. Fair enough. Its purpose is, after all, to sell or tell an idea, a product, a service, a message, or a story. Over time, society has created corridors within which advertising must travel. Legislatures and self-regulators acknowledge that advertising can be both subjective and objective and that some puffery and self-vaunting is to be accepted, but they have also taken steps to counter some of its harmful effects and to protect certain potentially vulnerable audiences.

In 1914, the offence of misleading advertising was added to the Criminal Code,[1] and 1960, Parliament added a provision to the Combines Investigation Act to combat misrepresentations regarding the regular price of goods.[2] In 1969, the Criminal Code provision was also transferred to the Combines Investigation Act,[3] and in 1976, the two sections were consolidated into a single provision,[4] which has been further transformed into a broader single section of the Competition Act that deals with commercial misrepresentations to the public.[5] On the self-regulatory side, the Canadian Advertising Foundation (CAF), now succeeded by Advertising Standards Canada (ASC), has administered the Canadian Code of Advertising Standards since 1963.[6]

In November 1970, in an inarguably innovative step, William Tetley, Quebec's minister of financial institutions, companies, and co-operatives, introduced Bill 45 in the National Assembly. The Consumer Protection Act, which became law on 14 July 1971, anticipated the authority of the governor in council "to determine standards for advertising goods, whether or not they are the object of a contract, or credit, especially all advertising intended for children."[7] Pursuant to that legislative authority, Quebec enacted a regulation that prohibited advertising directed at children, defined as persons under thirteen years of age, in a series of defined circumstances.

It was to be expected that the law would be challenged as it especially indisposed toy manufacturers and food-product companies, among others, that had designed products for children's consumption. These companies worried about loss of revenue and expressed concern that there would be a dramatic decline in the choice of programs offered to children if they no longer supported such programs with their advertising. Indeed, because the greatest share of advertising to children was on television, it was also to be expected that such a challenge would be lodged on the basis that such a prohibition constituted an interference with the federal government's plenary authority over broadcasting.

Such a challenge occurred when the food manufacturer Kellogg's ran an animated advertisement on television. Under the Consumer Protection Act regulation, no one may "use ... advertising intended for children which ... employs cartoons."[8] Quebec sought to invoke its regulatory authority against Kellogg's, which the company challenged in 1974 on the basis that the regulation exceeded the constitutional authority of the province. The decision was appealed from the Quebec Superior Court to the Court of Appeal and thence to the Supreme Court of Canada. The Supreme Court upheld the validity of that provision of the regulation, particularly as Quebec had applied it against an advertiser rather than against a broadcaster.[9]

In 1973, James A. McGrath, a member of parliament for St John's East in Newfoundland and Labrador, proposed a bill to prohibit the broadcast of commercial advertising during children's programs.[10] While the bill was not adopted, it gave rise to many debates and discussions and motivated public bodies to study advertising's potential effects on children. At the same time in Quebec, the Mouvement pour l'abolition de la publicité aux enfants, which had been set up in 1970, also exerted pressure in favour of stricter regulations concerning children.

In 1978, the Quebec legislature amended the Consumer Protection Act[11] and, while the substance of the children's advertising prohibition remained the same, changed the numbering of the relevant sections of the law and regulations.[12] More significantly, in 1989, Irwin Toy went before the Supreme Court of Canada with the intention to demonstrate that the Quebec legislation was unconstitutional. It failed. It challenged the constitutionality of the act on several grounds, including the alleged provincial legislative interference with freedom of expression. Important in the context of this book, in addressing the conflict with the federal government's plenary authority over broadcasting, the majority stated:

> On the whole, despite the fact that the relative impact on television advertising is much greater than it was in Kellogg's, we are of the opinion that ss. 248 and 249 of the Act, as modified by or completed by the regulations, can also be said to be legislation of general application enacted in relation to consumer protection, as in Kellogg's, rather than a colourable attempt, under the guise of a law of general application, to legislate in relation to television advertising. In other words, the dominant aspect of the law for purposes of characterization is the regulation of all forms of advertising directed at persons under thirteen years of age rather than the prohibition of television advertising which cannot be said to be the exclusive or even primary aim of the legislation.[13]

The validity of the prohibition in the Quebec Consumer Protection Act has not been subsequently challenged; nor is there any likelihood that it will be. Arguments are raised from time to time about whether broadcasters can provide Quebec children with the range of television programming that children outside Quebec receive because of the lack of revenue available to Quebec-based broadcasters from commercial advertising on such programs outside Quebec. However, this is a policy issue, one that depends on the government of Quebec of the day, and is unrelated to the constitutional authority of the province to curtail advertising directed at children.

THE REGULATION OF ADVERTISING DIRECTED TO CHILDREN

Advertising, particularly that directed to children, seems to be a perpetually controversial subject. There have been many concerns about, among other things, the effect television may have on the development and perceptions of young children. As the Supreme Court of Canada emphasized in *Quebec (Attorney General) v. Irwin Toy Limited*: "Generally, the concerns at the origin of the act and the voluntary regulation in this domain have to do with the special vulnerability of young children with respect to manipulation by media, their incapacity to distinguish fiction from reality or to grasp the persuasive intention carried by the message, and the secondary effects of external influences on the family and parental authority."[14]

In light of such concerns, in this chapter we will look at the legislation and regulatory codes with respect to advertising directed to children that have been adopted by regulatory bodies and the industry. In particular, we will study the substance of the regulation instituted by the Quebec Office de la protection du consommateur (OPC), the CBC, the CAB, and the ASC.

THE CONSUMER PROTECTION ACT, AS APPLIED BY THE OPC

One of the OPC's principal missions is to apply the Consumer Protection Act, which, in section 252, defines "to advertise" or "to make use of advertising" as "to prepare, utilize, distribute, publish or broadcast an advertisement, or to cause it to be distributed, published or broadcast." As noted above, sections 248 and 249 of the act prohibit advertising in Quebec directed at children under thirteen years of age:

> 248 Subject to what is provided in the regulations, no person may make use of commercial advertising directed at persons under thirteen years of age.
>
> 249 To determine whether or not an advertisement is directed at persons under thirteen years of age, account must be taken of the context of the presentation, and in particular of
>
> (a) the nature and intended purpose of the goods advertised;

(b) the manner of presenting such advertisement;
(c) the time and place it is shown.

The act allows for several exceptions to these regulations. Among other things, broadcasters are permitted to air an advertising message on television to promote a show intended for children, on the condition that such a message complies with certain requirements stated in the regulation. For example, a commercial message may not:

(a) exaggerate the nature, characteristics, performance or duration of goods or services ...
(e) directly incite a child to buy or to urge another person to buy goods or services or to seek information about it ...
(g) advertise goods or services that, because of their nature, quality or ordinary use, should not be used by children ...
(j) portray a person acting in an imprudent manner ...
(o) suggest that owning or using a product will develop in a child a physical, social or psychological advantage over other children of his age, or that being without the product will have the opposite effect;
(p) advertise goods in a manner misleading a child into think [*sic*] that, for the regular price of those goods, he can obtain goods other than those advertised.[15]

Thus, the Consumer Protection Act prohibits the advertising of products such as toys, sweets, food, and certain services during children's programs unless the commercial message is aimed, say, at parents rather than the young children.[16] The act also pays special attention to certain characteristics of advertising messages in order to determine whether they target children (as such techniques are prohibited). For example:

1 The use of themes relating to fantasy, magic, mystery, suspense or adventure.
2 The use of persons with whom a child can identify: the undue use of children, the use of children's voices, of heroes, of imaginary or fanciful creatures, and of animals. ...
5 The use of music which appeals particularly to children.[17]

This type of advertising is permitted in programs other than those for children on the condition that the content of the advertising message does not target children under thirteen years of age.

Moreover, the OPC has established directives applying to cases in which advertising is addressed equally to parents and children. Even this type of advertising may only be broadcast during programs for which children between two and eleven years of age make up less than 15 per cent of the audience.[18] There are also rules for advertising messages intended exclusively for children broadcast during programming that is not itself exclusively intended for children. Such commercial messages may only be broadcast during programs for which children make up less than 5 per cent of the audience. In the case of a new program or a program schedule change, the OPC provides that advertisers must carefully consider the following criteria in order to comply with the above-mentioned directives: "(1) the type of program, (2) the time of broadcasting, (3) competition from other programs at the same time, and (4) the data on viewing levels."[19] Note that the act targets only commercial advertising. Educational advertising is permitted, but must comply with certain conditions that will not be discussed here.

The provisions of Quebec's Consumer Protection Act cannot be applied to signals that originate outside of Quebec and are received by Quebec residents via broadcast distribution undertakings. Thus, advertising messages from English Canada and the United States delivered on cable or satellite platforms are not subject to these regulations.

THE CBC PROGRAM POLICY ON ADVERTISING

In 1975, the CBC, on the basis of an agreement with the CRTC, adopted a policy prohibiting the broadcast of advertising messages intended for children during its programming. As a result, certain programs on CBC television may not be sponsored or interrupted by advertising messages. According to the 1996 version of the CBC program policy 1.1.11, "Programming Not Eligible for Commercial Content," the following types of programs may not be sponsored or interrupted for commercials: "national and provincial school broadcasts" and "programs directed to children under 13 years of age." The only advertising messages which may be broadcast are billboards, that is, those intended only to identify the show's sponsor (by name, but not by image), a role makers or designers of children's products are not allowed to fill.[20] In this respect, the CBC has chosen to adopt standards stricter than those followed by private broadcasters.[21]

In September 2002, the CBC's "Commercial Impact" program policy came into effect. The CBC argues that, since its mandate is subject to economic constraints, it has no choice but to engage in commercial activity in its programming. In general, it "accepts product placement in some of its programs, provided that it stays within the bounds of good taste, respects CBC/Radio-Canada values such as openness, and does not affect the quality of the broadcast."[22] This clause also applies to the placement of products intended for parents in children's programs. In Quebec, Radio-Canada is still fully subject to OPC regulations in this respect.

THE ADVERTISING STANDARDS CANADA CODE OF ADVERTISING STANDARDS

In 1963, the Canadian advertising industry adopted a set of self-regulatory guidelines on advertising, namely, the Canadian Code of Advertising Standards.[23] The code, which has been revised regularly over the course of its lifetime, is published by the ASC, which administers it jointly with its regional councils. The majority of advertisers, advertising agencies, media that carry advertising, and suppliers that participate in the advertising process endorse the code.

In its revised 2007 version, the Canadian Code of Advertising Standards defines advertising as "any message (the content of which is controlled directly or indirectly by the advertiser) expressed in any language and communicated in any medium (except those listed under Exclusions) to Canadians with the intent to influence their choice, opinion or behaviour." It establishes guidelines that apply to how products and services can be advertised, but not to which products and services can advertised. As the code explains under the heading "Scope of the Code," "The authority of the Code applies only to the content of advertisements and does not prohibit the promotion of legal products or services or their portrayal in circumstances of normal use."

The latest version of the code includes two provisions that directly concern children:

> 12 Advertising to Children
> Advertising that is directed to children must not exploit their credulity, lack of experience or their sense of loyalty, and must not present information or illustrations that might result in their physical, emotional or moral harm ...
> 13 Advertising to Minors
> Products prohibited from sale to minors must not be advertised in such a way as to appeal particularly to persons under legal age, and people featured in advertisements for such products must be, and clearly seen to be, adults under the law.

The code also states that the Broadcast Code for Advertising to Children will regulate broadcast advertising directed to children in English Canada.[24]

A committee specially established by the ASC meets regularly to evaluate and pre-screen advertising messages. When messages comply with the code's requirements, the committee assigns them a clearance number. Broadcasters are responsible for broadcasting only advertising messages that have received clearance numbers.

The ASC's standards division handles complaints concerning all national English-language advertising and all advertising in Ontario. Its French-language counterpart, the Conseil des normes de la publicité, handles national French-language advertising and advertising originating in Quebec. Regional councils address complaints about English-language advertising in their respective regions.

THE CAB'S BROADCASTING CODE FOR ADVERTISING TO CHILDREN

In 1973, the CRTC asked private broadcasters to comply with the provisions of the CAB's Broadcast Code for Advertising to Children. The following year, the CRTC imposed compliance with this code as a condition of licence for all broadcast licensees (including conventional and specialty services, but not pay-television licensees, which are prohibited from broadcasting advertising during their programming).

However, it only applies in English Canada since, as discussed above, Quebec prohibits advertising to children during children's programs.

The children's advertising division of ASC, the Children's Clearance Committee, administers this code. The ASC published its first *Ad Complaints Report*, which discusses complaints, their resolution, and considerable additional information, in 1997. It has published annual reports since then and has long included quarterly reports as well.[25]

In 2003, the ASC revised the Broadcasting Code for Advertising to Children. The most recent version of the code stipulates that its purpose is: "To guide advertisers and agencies in preparing commercial messages that adequately recognize the special characteristics of the children's audience. Children, especially the very young, live in a world that is part imaginary, part real and sometimes do not distinguish clearly between the two. Children's advertising should respect and not abuse the power of the child's imagination."

The code addresses certain types of advertising messages in particular. It states: "'A child directed message' refers to a commercial message on behalf of a product or service for which children are the only users or form a substantial part of the market as users, and the message (i.e. language, selling points, visuals) is presented in a manner that is directed primarily to children."[26]

Some of the provisions of the code that are more relevant to children are as follows:

> 3 Factual Presentation
>
> (a) No children's advertising may employ any device or technique that attempts to transmit messages below the threshold of normal awareness.
>
> (b) Written, sound, photographic and other visual presentations must not exaggerate service, product or premium characteristics, such as performance, speed, size, colour, durability, etc. ...
>
> (d) When children's advertising shows results from a drawing, construction, craft or modelling toy or kit, the results should be reasonably attainable by an average child.
>
> 4 Product Prohibitions
>
> (a) Products not intended for use by children advertised either directly or through promotions that are primarily child-oriented. ...

5 Avoiding Undue Pressure

(a) Children's advertising must not directly urge children to purchase or urge them to ask their parents to make inquiries or purchases. ...

6 Scheduling

(a) The same commercial message or more than one commercial message promoting the same product cannot be aired more than once in a half-hour children's program. In children's programs of longer duration, the same commercial message or more than one commercial message promoting the same product must not appear more than once in any half-hour period.

(b) No station or network may carry more than four minutes of commercial messages in any one half-hour of children's programming or more than an average of eight minutes per hour in children's programs of longer duration. ...

7 Promotion by Program Characters, Advertiser-Generated Characters, and Personal Endorsement ...

(c) Professional actors, actresses or announcers who are not identified with characters in programs appealing to children may be used as spokespersons in advertising directed to children.

(d) Puppets, persons and characters well-known to children may present factual and relevant generic statements about nutrition, safety, education, etc. in children's advertising.

8 Price and Purchase Terms ...

(d) When more than one toy is featured in a commercial message it must be made clear in audio and video which toys are sold separately (this includes accessories).

9 Comparison Claims ...

(b) In the case of toys or children's possessions, comparisons should not be made with the previous year's model, even when the statements or claims are valid.

10 Safety ...

(b) Commercial messages must not show products being used in an unsafe or dangerous manner. (e.g. tossing a food item into the air and attempting to catch it in the mouth, etc.).

11 Social Values

(a) Children's advertising must not encourage or portray a

range of values that are inconsistent with the moral, ethical or legal standards of contemporary Canadian society.

Although they are not strictly speaking a part of it, there are guidelines and procedures appended to the code to provide broadcasters, advertisers, advertising agencies, and media representatives with guidance concerning certain clauses.[27] For example, one of the guidelines concerns advertising directed to pre-school children: "Children of pre-school age often are unable to distinguish between program content and advertisements. Therefore, any commercial message scheduled for viewing during the school-day morning hours should be directed to the family, parent or an adult, rather than to children and should have the requisite ASC clearance number if appearing in or adjacent to a child-directed program."

In April 2004, a new version of the code included a set of interpretation guidelines concerning food advertising directed at children.[28] These guidelines include the requirement that "snack foods are clearly presented as such, not as substitutes for meals." They apply across Canada (except for Quebec, where advertising to children is prohibited).

In 2005, the *Children's Broadcast Advertising Clearance Guide* was published. Its purpose is to "help advertisers, advertising agencies and broadcasters develop, schedule and present commercials that comply with the CAB Broadcast Code for Advertising to Children (Children's Code)." In 2007, four new rules for clause 11 were added to the interpretation guidelines, as follows:

ii Every "child-directed message" for a product or service should encourage responsible use of the advertised product or service with a view toward the healthy development of the child.
iii Advertising of food products should not discourage or disparage healthy lifestyle choices or the consumption of fruits or vegetables or other foods recommended for increased consumption in Canada's Food Guide, and Health Canada's nutrition policies and recommendations applicable to children under 12.
iv The amount of food product featured in a "child-directed message" should not be excessive or more than would be reasonable to acquire, use or, where applicable, consume, by a person in the situation depicted.

v If an advertisement depicts food being consumed by a person in the advertisement, or suggests that the food will be consumed, the quantity of food shown should not exceed the labelled serving size on the Nutrition Facts Panel (where no such serving size is applicable, the quantity of food shown should not exceed a single serving size that would be appropriate for consumption by a person of the age depicted).

All broadcasters that are ASC members (except for those in Quebec, where advertising to children is prohibited) have agreed to conform to the code. Moreover, they have agreed to submit their advertising messages to the ASC Children's Clearance Committee for evaluation. If the committee finds that an advertising message complies with the code, it issues it a clearance number, which gives broadcasters permission to broadcast the message.

ADVERTISING TO CHILDREN IN CANADA: A REFERENCE GUIDE

In 2006, the CAB, the ASC, the ACA, and the Institute of Communications and Advertising (ICA) published a revised version of their reference guide, *Advertising to Children in Canada*.[29] The guide was designed to encourage the development of responsible advertising and promote self-regulation in all forms of media. In its introductory language, it declares its purpose:

- To increase awareness and understanding of the role of regulation of advertising to children in Canada, including food advertising, through examination of the codes in place, including the required preclearance process of all television advertising prior to going on air (except in Quebec).
- To build more public confidence about the advertising regulations in place, the process for complaint and review, and how this system protects children.
- To examine the role of the CCA whose strategy it is to create and implement initiatives that will educate, empower and benefit the children of Canada, as the credible, caring and authori-

tative voice of responsible children's advertising and communications.[30]

GUIDELINES FOR ADVERTISING TO CHILDREN AND ADOLESCENTS IN THE CMA CODE OF ETHICS AND STANDARDS OF PRACTICE

In its Code of Ethics and Standards of Practice,[31] the Canadian Marketing Association (CMA) provides its members with guidelines for advertising that targets children and adolescents. These rules apply to all media. Here are the main provisions:

K1 Age
For purposes of this Code, the term child refers to someone who has not reached his or her 13th birthday.
K2 Responsibility
Marketing to children imposes a special responsibility on marketers. Marketers must recognize that children are not adults and that not all marketing techniques are appropriate for children.
K3 Consent
When marketing to persons between 13 years and the age of majority, marketers are strongly cautioned that children may be exposed to these communications and, in such cases, these interactions with children are governed by the following guidelines concerning consent. See also Section L3 of this Code regarding Consent in Marketing to Teenagers.

K3.1 Except as provided for below in Section K4 of this Code, Contests Directed to Children, all marketing interactions directed to children that include the collection, transfer and requests for personal information require the opt-in consent of the child's parent or guardian.

K3.2 Where the child, parent or guardian withdraws or declines permission to collect, use or disclose a child's information, marketers must immediately delete all such information from their database.

K4 Contests Directed to Children
Subject to applicable laws, marketers may collect personal information from children for the purposes of contests without obtain-

ing the parent or guardian's opt-in consent, only if the marketer:

- collects a minimal amount of personal information, sufficient only to determine the winner(s);
- deals only with the winner(s)' parent or guardian and does not contact the winner(s);
- does not retain the personal information following the conclusion of the contest or sweepstakes;
- makes no use of the personal information other than to determine the contest or sweepstakes winner(s); and
- does not transfer or make available the personal information to any other individual or organization.

K5 Credulity
Marketing to children must not exploit children's credulity, lack of experience or sense of loyalty.
K6 Age-Appropriate Language
When marketing to children, marketing communications must be age appropriate and presented in simple language, easily understood by children.
K7 Commercial Transactions
Marketers must not knowingly accept an order from a child without a parent or guardian's opt-in consent. Marketers must not pressure a child to urge their parents or guardians to purchase a product or service.

Finally, with respect to teenagers, standards similar to those for children aged thirteen and under have been established, taking into consideration the market with which this age group is associated:

L1 Age and Application
For the purpose of this Code, the term teenager refers to someone who has reached their 13th birthday but has not yet reached the age of majority in their province or territory of residence.
These guidelines do not apply to teenagers living independently of their parents or guardians and who by federal, provincial or territorial statute or regulation are deemed to be adults.
L2 Responsibility
Marketing to teenagers imposes special responsibilities on mar-

keters. Marketers will use discretion and sensitivity in marketing to teenagers, to address the age, knowledge, sophistication and maturity of teenagers. Marketers should exercise caution that they do not take advantage of or exploit teenagers.

L2.1 Marketers must not portray sexual behaviour or violence that is inconsistent with community or industry standards.

L2.2 Marketers must respect the parent/guardian-teenager relationship and must not encourage the teenager to exclude parents or guardians from a purchase decision.

L2.3 Marketers must not solicit, collect or knowingly use personal information from teenagers as a means of acquiring further household information.

L3 Consent

This section enables marketers to establish communication with teenagers in defined stages, according to the sensitivity or type of information, the teenager's age and the nature of the consent to be provided.

L3.1 Marketers must obtain the opt-in consent from a teenager under the age of 16 for the collection and use of their contact information. See *Glossary of Terms* of this Code for a definition of "contact information."

Marketers must obtain the opt-in consent of the parent or guardian prior to the disclosure of a teenager's contact information to a third party.

Marketers must obtain the opt-in consent of the parent or guardian for the collection, use or disclosure of personal information of a teenager under the age of 16.

L3.2 Marketers must obtain the opt-in consent from the teenager for the collection, use and disclosure of their personal information.

L3.3 Where the teenager, parent or guardian withdraws or declines the permission required to collect, use or disclose a teenager's information, marketers must immediately delete all such information from their database ...

L4 Exposure to Children

When marketing to teenagers, marketers are strongly cautioned that children may be exposed to these communications and in such cases, these interactions with children are governed by the guidelines concerning consent in Section K of this Code, *Special Considerations in Marketing to Children*.

L5 Credulity

Marketing to teenagers must not unduly exploit teenagers' impressionability, or susceptibility to peer or social pressures. Marketers must not imply that possession or use of a product or service will make its owner superior to others, or that without it the individual will be open to ridicule or contempt.

L6 Age-Appropriate Language

Marketers must use language that is age-appropriate and easy to understand when marketing to teenagers.

L7 Commercial Transactions

Marketers must be aware that transactions with teenagers may not be legally enforceable against the teenager, or his or her parent or guardian.

OTHER STAKEHOLDERS

In Canada, a number of organizations play an influential role in regulating advertising directed at children. We will discuss Concerned Children's Advertisers and the Quebec Coalition on Weight-Related Problems, along with the CRTC regulations concerning advertising for alcoholic beverages, in the following sections.

Concerned Children's Advertisers

In 1990, the not-for-profit Concerned Children's Advertisers (CCA) was established in order to provide a "credible, caring and authoritative voice" on responsible advertising directed at children.[32] Its members are private companies that operate in the child and family markets. CCA encourages compliance with the Broadcasting Code for Advertising to Children; to this end it, sits on the ASC Children's Clearance Committee, which screens advertising for children and provides preclearance where warranted. Above all, CCA is recognized for having produced, in partnership with Health Canada, nearly forty public service messages on topics as child safety, physical health, self-esteem, drug abuse, bullying, abuse, and media literacy.[33] Through its announcements, CCA has three objectives:

- Help children to better deal with issues of challenge in their lives;
- Support parents in the healthy development of their children; and
- Support educators, community, and health care workers in the teaching of media literacy and life skills.

Consistent with these objectives, in 2005, CCA launched the Long Live Kids initiative, which consists in a series of public service announcements and an educational program for teachers, parents, and community leaders in Canada. The initiative has three phases:

- Phase I: Healthier eating;
- Phase II: Increased physical activity; and
- Phase III: Improved media literacy.

The third phase launched in February 2010, and encourages children to improve their critical thinking skills with respect to the messages that they receive from all media in order to help them make informed, healthy choices.

The Quebec Coalition on Weight-Related Problems

Since 1990, the Coalition contre la publicité aux enfants, composed of a number of consumer associations and the OPC, had attempted to pressure the CRTC so that Quebec's Consumer Protection Act could be applied to signals that originated outside of Quebec but were rebroadcast within it by cable or satellite operators. According to the coalition, the absence of such a requirement was counterproductive to all other positive measures.

The Quebec Coalition on Weight-Related Problems (the Weight Coalition) joined this cause and has been acting on the provincial level since 2006 by encouraging the establishment of public policies designed to counteract and prevent weight problems. Thus, in its manifesto, the Weight Coalition pressured the federal and Quebec governments to act to, for example, create a healthier socio-cultural environment, especially with respect to media and advertising.

According to the Weight Coalition, the provisions of the Consumer Protection Act cannot really protect Quebec children from advertising: "On one hand because there is no systematic oversight of compliance with or strict enforcement of the regulations, and on the other hand because the wording of the provisions, which is more than 25 years old, is no longer consistent with today's reality."[34]

The Weight Coalition thus advocates for the amendment of the regulation on advertising to children. It monitors the effectiveness of the regulatory approach, and since 2007 it has submitted advertising messages to the OPC for examination.[35] While the advertising does not directly target children, in some cases the Weight Coalition was apparently testing the limits of the prohibition against commercial advertising to children under the age of thirteen. It has aimed to test the limitations of the legislation and to get the OPC to define the parameters more clearly in present-day terms.

CRTC Regulations that Concern Advertising for Alcoholic Beverages

Broadcast advertising of alcoholic beverages has been regulated since the mid-1930s.[36] As an aside, there was the long-standing irony that, since 1928, it had been illegal for consumers to transport wine, beer, or spirits purchased in one province to another, or for wineries to ship directly to consumers in other provinces.[37] When Bill C-311 became law on 28 June 2012, that prohibition finally disappeared.[38]

Today, the CRTC continues to stipulate that it must approve messages advertising alcohol before they can be broadcast.[39] Since 1986, it has done this by applying the Code for Broadcast Advertising of Alcoholic Beverages.[40] In 1994, in accordance with recommendations made by the Alcoholic Beverage Broadcast Advertising Advisory Committee in 1994,[41] it clarified the code. In the latest version, dating from 1996, three provisions now refer to children and state that advertising for alcohol must not:

> (b) be directed at persons under the legal drinking age, associate any such product with youth or youth symbols, or portray persons under the legal drinking age or persons who could reasonably be mistaken for such persons in a context where any such product is being shown or promoted;
> (c) portray the product in the context of, or in relation to, an activity attractive primarily to people under the legal drinking age;
> (d) contain an endorsement of the product, personally or by implication, either directly or indirectly, by any person, character

> or group who is or is likely to be a role model for minors because of a past or present position of public trust, special achievement in any field of endeavour, association with charities and/or advocacy activities benefiting children, reputation or exposure in the mass media.[42]

An interpretive section, which is not part of the code, includes the following explanations:

> With reference to paragraph (b):
> The message should be overtly directed to persons who are of the legal drinking age in the province where the message is broadcast. No such message should depict, under any circumstances, children, children's toys, children's clothing, playground equipment, or wading pools. Objects that are commonly used by children, but not considered childish when used by adults (e.g. most sports equipment, Frisbees and colouring pencils) may be depicted in such messages. Mythical or fairy tale characters appealing to children, such as Santa Claus, the Tooth Fairy, the Easter Bunny or Halloween characters and symbols, should not be depicted in such messages under any circumstance.
> With reference to paragraph (c):
> The product should not be portrayed in the context of, or in relation to, for example, a performance, event or activity where the audience or the participants are expected to be predominantly people under the legal drinking age or where the television or film audiences of the featured performer(s) consist predominantly of people under the legal drinking age.
> With reference to paragraph (d):
> Once established as a role model for minors, a person will be considered to remain a role model for a period of 10 years from the date of retirement from the activity.

As we have discussed in this chapter, there are legislative, regulatory, and self-regulatory laws, codes, and standards that prohibit or provide a framework for television advertising to which children might be exposed. In the next part, we will discuss film, video, and video game environments.

PART TWO

Film and Video

There are generally few statistics on film attendance in Canada for children aged two to eleven; however, North American data show that group accounts for 15 per cent of moviegoers and 11 per cent of cinema tickets sold although it makes up 14 per cent of the population. The twelve-to-seventeen age group represents 8 per cent of the population, 10 per cent of moviegoers, and 13 per cent of tickets sold.[1] Altogether, those aged twenty-four and younger buy nearly 50 per cent of the tickets sold in the United States and Canada.

Television and film viewing habits and practices changed when video recorders and DVD players came onto the market, although, interestingly, the number of Canadian homes with video recorders dropped from 87 per cent to 79 per cent between 1997 and 2007.[2] The decrease was probably a consequence of DVD player purchases, since their presence in Canadian homes rose from 20 to 85 per cent between 2001 and 2007. These statistics reveal the importance of entertainment in Canadian society.

In the following sections, we will lay out the different film and video classification systems in force in Canada. Then, we will describe in greater detail the unique circumstances of the Régie du cinéma classification system.

6

Film Boards

PROVINCIAL FILM CLASSIFICATION SYSTEMS

In Canada, the regulation of motion pictures falls under provincial jurisdiction. Six different film boards cover nine provinces (some of which share boards).[1] Since 1997, for example, British Columbia's Business Practices and Consumer Protection Authority (BPCPA) has also classified films for Saskatchewan, even though Saskatchewan has its own Film and Video Classification Board. The Yukon has no film classification system; it applies British Columbia's regulations. In the Northwest Territories and Nunavut, there is legislation that requires film classification, but no film board. Instead, both territories use Alberta's film classification system. Prince Edward Island and New Brunswick use Nova Scotia's film classification system under the Maritime Film Classification Board, which they formed in 1995. For French-language films, New Brunswick uses Quebec's classification system.

In addition to a classification system, each film board has provisions that can exempt certain films from any rating. The exemptions differ from province to province; for example, some provinces have adopted policies that authorize their film boards to refuse to classify films with content they consider inappropriate for viewing. Note that all of the provinces authorize stamping film packages with both advisories and classification categories. Finally, all of the provinces permit the appeal of film classification decisions.

PROVINCIAL VIDEO CLASSIFICATION SYSTEMS

Seven provinces (Saskatchewan, Manitoba, Ontario, Quebec, Nova Scotia, New Brunswick, and Prince Edward Island) require videos to be categorized according to a classification system. As in the case of film classification systems, New Brunswick and Prince Edward Island use the Maritime Film Classification Board system. Seven provinces (British Columbia, Saskatchewan, Manitoba, Quebec, Nova Scotia, New Brunswick, and Prince Edward Island) have adopted video labelling systems. In those provinces, all video packaging is labelled with a sticker that advises viewers of advisories assigned by the regional film board. Alberta and Ontario do not have video labelling systems.

THE CANADIAN MOTION PICTURE DISTRIBUTORS ASSOCIATION'S CANADIAN HOME VIDEO RATING SYSTEM

The six Canadian film boards do not all operate under the same film classification system, and both the system and the classification categories differ from one board to the next. Nonetheless, major classification changes in recent years have resulted in the practical need to harmonize the classification of home video products across all provinces (except Quebec). This has been accomplished in the following way.

Principal credit for the standardization goes to the Motion Picture Association – Canada (MPA), formerly the Canadian Motion Picture Distributors Association, a group that represents the major American studios in Canada.[2] Since 1995, it has established and administered the Canadian Home Video Rating System (CHVRS), which categorizes videos and DVDs for home consumption. After the provinces have classified a production according to their respective systems, the MPA revises the provincial classifications and averages them, using the CHVRS to provide a final standard classification for the entire Canadian home video market. The CHVRS has six categories:

G: Suitable for viewing by all ages.
PG: Parental guidance advised. Themes or content may not be suitable for children.

14A: Suitable for people 14 years of age or older. Those under 14 should view with an adult. No rental or purchase by those under 14. Parents cautioned. May contain violence, coarse language and/or sexually suggestive scenes.
18A: Suitable for people 18 years of age or older. Persons under 18 should view with an adult. No rental or purchase by those under 18. Parents strongly cautioned. Will likely contain: explicit violence; frequent coarse language; sexual activity; and/or horror.
R: Restricted to 18 years and over. No rental or purchase by those under 18. Content not suitable for minors. Video contains frequent use of: sexual activity; brutal/graphic violence; intense horror; and/or other disturbing content.
E: Exempt. Contains material not subject to classification such as documentaries, nature, travel, music, arts and culture, sports and educational and instructional information.[3]

The MPA also provides a set of sixteen descriptions of the general definitions of information pieces that may be used when classifying films: not recommended for young children, not recommended for children, frightening scenes, mature theme, coarse language, crude content, nudity, sexual content, violence, disturbing content, substance abuse, gory scenes, explicit sexual content, brutal violence, sexual violence, and language may offend.[4]

Except for Quebec, all of the provinces comply with the CHVRS on a voluntary basis. This means they have adapted their film classification systems to be consistent with the CHVRS categories. Figure 6.1 summarizes the different film and video classification systems used in Canada.

QUEBEC'S RÉGIE DU CINÉMA

In Quebec, the Cinema Act established a regulatory organization, the Régie du cinéma, which is responsible for governing and monitoring film.[5] The Régie classifies films and issues licences to distributors, movie theatre operators, and video retailers. It also ensures that motion picture distribution and use rights are respected.

The Régie's film policy applies to all areas of activity relating to film, including production, distribution, public presentations, and

	FILM CLASSIFICATION IN CANADA	HOME VIDEO
British Columbia	G, PG, 14A, 18A, R, A	G, DP, 14A, 18A, R, E
Alberta	G, PG, 14A, 18A, R	
Saskatchewan	G, PG, 14A, 18A, R, A	
Manitoba	G, PG, 14A, 18A, R, E	
Ontario	G, PG, 14A, 18A, R	
Nova Scotia	G, PG, 14A, 18A, R, A	
Prince Edward Island	G, PG, 14A, 18A, R, A	
New Brunswick	G, PG, 14A, 18A, R, A	
Newfoundland and Labrador	G, PG, 14A, 18A, R, A	
Quebec	G GENERAL, 13 ANS+, 16 ANS+, 18 ANS+	
Northwest Territories	G, PG, 14A, 18A, R	N/A
Yukon	G, PG, 14A, 18A, R, A	N/A
Nunavut	G, PG, 14A, 18A, R	N/A

Figure 6.1 Film and video classification systems used in Canada

the retail video trade. The policy has a number of objectives, such as the "establishment of mechanisms to oversee the production, exhibition and distribution of such works."[6] We will focus on this objective since it explains why the régie has established a film classification system.

Sections 76 and 76.1 of Quebec's Cinema Act specify the conditions under which a stamp (a form of label or sticker) is required. Generally, a Régie stamp is required for every film presented in public and for every film sold, rented, shared, or exchanged commercially. Section 81 explains the Régie's film classification process. It establishes Quebec's classification categories and some of the conditions placed on the Régie's agreement to classify films. If the Régie believes that a film's content does not interfere with public order, and in particular, that it does not promote or condone sexual violence, it classifies the film under one of the following categories:

> 1 "For all," if it considers that the film may be viewed by persons of all ages;
> 2 "13 and over," if it considers that the film may be viewed only by persons 13 years of age or older;
> 3 "16 and over," if it considers that the film may be viewed only by persons 16 years of age or older;
> 4 "18 and over," if it considers that the film may be viewed only by persons 18 years of age or older.

Section 86 provides related prohibitions:

> No person may admit to the public exhibition of a film,
> 1 a person under 13 years of age who is not accompanied by a person of full age, if the film is classified "13 and over";
> 2 a person under 16 years of age, if the film is classified "16 and over";
> 3 a person under 18 years of age, if the film is classified "18 and over."

Similar restrictions apply to videos:

> No person may, in a video material retail outlet, sell, lease or lend video material to, or exchange such material with, a person
> 1 who is under 13 years of age, if the film is classified "13 and over";
> 2 who is under 16 years of age, if the film is classified "16 and over";
> 3 who is under 18 years of age, if the film is classified "18 years and over";

4 who is under 18 years of age, if the film consists primarily of scenes of explicit sexual activity and is the object of a filing certificate issued by the régie before 15 June 1992.[7]

The Régie can refuse to classify films that it decides are contrary to public order or good morals.[8]

The Regulation Respecting Licences to Operate Premises Where Films Are Exhibited to the Public, Distributors' Licences and Video Material Retail Dealers' Licences[9] sets out a number of rights and obligations, including those stated in sections 17, 18, and 26, which specify that the licence holder of a permit to operate an establishment where films are presented to the public must post the Régie du cinéma classification for each film. Such licensees, like holders of distribution licences, must indicate the classification category and, if applicable, the Régie's remarks, indications, and description of the film. The published classification category has to comply with the model stamps issued by the Régie.

Moreover, in order to protect youth, the regulations state that video retail licence holders have only three ways to present adult material (which contains scenes of explicit sex or extreme violence): (1) in an area reserved for such videos with dividers that do not allow the contents of the display to be seen clearly and that is advertised by a sign that reads "ADULTS"; (2) on a shelf or automatic distributor so that only the titles of the films are visible; (3) in a catalogue placed out of public sight or in the area reserved for adult video cassettes. Posters for such films must fulfil the same requirements as the catalogue. Licence holders must also use the Régie's advisory material so that the public will be aware of the category assigned to the film.

PART THREE

Video Games

Since the mid-1980s, video games have played a growing role in the lives of children and adolescents. In fact, today, the video game industry is the fastest growing part of the entertainment sector, having overtaken the film and music industries. According to the Entertainment Software Association of Canada (ESAC), 47 per cent of Canadian homes have at least one video game console and 96 per cent have a computer.[1] Furthermore, nine out of ten children aged six to twelve were reported to have had played video games in the last four weeks, as were eight out of ten adolescents aged thirteen to seventeen. In both age groups, more than one out of three people played every day. Nonetheless, the average age of Canadian video game players is thirty-three.

7

The History of the Regulation of Video Games

THE EMERGENCE OF VIDEO GAME CLASSIFICATION SYSTEMS

When video games moved into the 16-bit era in the late 1980s, content realism increased dramatically. Graphic and sound quality made violent scenes, in particular those with a great deal of blood, far more explicit than during the 8-bit years, when images were much less realistic. Controversy that resulted from the realism of the content of some games led to a series of hearings in the United States in 1992 and 1993. As a result of these hearings, the video game industry was given one year to develop its own classification system, failing which the United States government would impose one.

Various classification boards quickly appeared. Notably, Sega of America launched its Videogame Rating Council (VRC) in 1993 to classify all Sega console-compatible video games according to three age categories (GA, MA-13, and MA-17);[1] however, the VRC was criticized by consumer groups and many media outlets for its perceived inconsistency and lack of clarity and Sega phased it out in 1994.[2] The same year, the 3DO Company unveiled its 3DO Rating System for games designed for its console. It had four age categories (E, 12, 17, and AO), but it too was phased out in 1994 when the ESRB took over the rating process.

In 1994, the Software Publishers Association (SPA) with the help of the Association of Shareware Professionals (ASP) created the Recreational Software Advisory Council (RSAC), an American organization.

Unlike the VRC and 3DO classification systems, the RSAC's labelling system was based on content rather than age. According to the SPA and ASP, this would allow parents to make their own decisions about what their children could see; however, the RSAC system was criticized for this very reason, especially since it applied only to computer software and not to video games for consoles. The RSAC shut down in 1999.[3]

THE ENTERTAINMENT SOFTWARE ASSOCIATION'S ENTERTAINMENT SOFTWARE RATING BOARD

In April 1994, a group of video game companies in the United States set up the Interactive Digital Software Association (IDSA), which in 2003 was renamed the Entertainment Software Association (ESA). The ESA has a Canadian branch: the Entertainment Software Association of Canada (ESAC). In July 1994, the IDSA proposed the Entertainment Software Rating Board (ESRB) to the United States Congress. The proposal was approved, and that September, the ESRB was established as the de facto evaluator of video games in the United States.

As a self-regulatory organization, the ESRB aimed to assign age and content ratings to video games, strengthen industry advertising guidelines, and provide responsible protection for online privacy with respect to consoles and computers in the United States and Canada.[4] Since 1994, the ESRB's classification system has grown from five to seven categories. According to the most recent version, updated in 2005, the system is as follows:

> Early Childhood: Titles rated EC (Early Childhood) have content that may be suitable for ages 3 and older. Contains no material that parents would find inappropriate.
> Everyone: Titles rated E (Everyone) have content that may be suitable for ages 6 and older. Titles in this category may contain minimal cartoon, fantasy or mild violence and/or infrequent use of mild language.
> Everyone 10+: Titles rated E10+ (Everyone 10 and older) have content that may be suitable for ages 10 and older. Titles in this category may contain more cartoon, fantasy or mild violence, mild language and/or minimal suggestive themes.
> Teen: Titles rated T (Teen) have content that may be suitable for ages 13 and older. Titles in this category may contain violence,

suggestive themes, crude humor, minimal blood, simulated gambling, and/or infrequent use of strong language.

Mature: Titles rated M (Mature) have content that may be suitable for persons ages 17 and older. Titles in this category may contain intense violence, blood and gore, sexual content and/or strong language.

Adults Only: Titles rated AO (Adults Only) have content that should only be played by persons 18 years and older. Titles in this category may include prolonged scenes of intense violence and/or graphic sexual content and nudity.

Rating Pending: Titles designated as RP (Rating Pending) have not yet been assigned a final ESRB rating. This icon appears only in advertising, marketing and promotional materials related to a game that is expected to carry an ESRB rating. The RP is replaced by a game's rating once it has been assigned.[5]

In addition to receiving a rating, each video game receives content descriptors that concern in particular whether the game portrays violence, blood, offensive language, sexuality, nudity, or drug or alcohol use.

Three evaluators who assign a rating initially determine video game classifications. ESRB staff then review the content and send a rating certificate to the publisher. The publisher can publish the game with the initial rating, or rework and resubmit it with the goal of obtaining a different rating. When a game is released with a certain rating, the ESRB can fine its publisher if consumers complain that the content and rating do not match. While the ESRB's video game classification is strictly voluntary, most publishers submit games for evaluation because many stores refuse to sell unrated games. Moreover, major console manufacturers do not grant licences to games to be used with their technology if such games have not received an ESRB-approved rating.

In 2004, the Retail Council of Canada (RCC) and ESAC jointly launched the Commitment to Parents initiative.[6] Video game retailers that participate in the program voluntarily commit to refusing to sell or rent games rated M (mature) or AO (adults only) to anyone under seventeen or eighteen years of age, respectively.[7] According to ESAC, 83 per cent of Canadian parents check the ESRB rating symbol before buying or renting a game for their children, and 88 per cent check the content advisory.[8]

Over the years, the ESRB has been accused of giving certain video games too low a rating. In Canada, British Columbia and Ontario both had to employ their film rating systems to ensure that *Soldier of Fortune* (2000) and *Manhunt* (2003) received ratings that restricted sales to adults only. Some Canadian provinces have nonetheless amended their film and video classification legislation to include the ESRB's system. In March 2005, the Ontario Film Review Board adopted it.[9] In April of the same year, the Maritime Film Classification Board did too, which means that the ESRB system applies in Nova Scotia, New Brunswick, and Prince Edward Island. In June 2005, Manitoba similarly included the ESRB's classification system in its new regulations.[10] Saskatchewan's Film and Video Classification Act did likewise in March 2006.[11] In November 2009, Alberta replaced its obsolete Amusement Act with the Film and Video Classification Act, which recognizes the ESRB's role with respect to classification.[12] In 2009, Quebec's Régie du cinéma published the guide *My Child and the Screen*, which also endorses the ESRB.[13]

In 2011, the ESRB rated 1,332 titles, divided as follows:

45 per cent received an E (everyone) rating
20 per cent received an E10+ (everyone age ten and up) rating
26 per cent received a T (teen) rating
9 per cent received an M (mature) rating

To avoid legislation, the videogame industry has made several attempts to devise video game self-regulatory codes. At the same time, governmental agencies have taken initiatives to better inform parents and protect children in the rapidly evolving video game environment. While these initiatives have provided useful guidelines, there is still no uniform regulatory approach, and the solutions remain quite disparate among the Canadian provinces and American states.

PART FOUR

The Internet

When the Internet arrived in Canadian homes in the 1990s, it revolutionized the definition, perception, and functions of media. The new medium made it possible for people to experience a wide variety of alphanumeric, audio, and video content. According to a report by Statistics Canada, in 2010, 80 per cent of Canadians aged sixteen and over used the Internet for personal purposes.[1] Another report, *Canadian Internet Use Survey*, stated that almost all users aged sixteen and over said they used the Internet from home. Among those under thirty, more than half said they went on the Internet to download or watch television shows and films.[2]

A CRTC report from 2006 showed that more and more young Canadians were on the Internet.[3] Indeed, from 2000 to 2006, the number of children aged twelve to fourteen who used the Internet weekly went from 85 to 95 per cent. Among those aged fifteen to nineteen, use rose from 81 to 96 per cent. There are very few recent studies done on children in the two-to-seven and eight-to-twelve age ranges. Two, one conducted in 2004 and entitled *Canada Online*[4] and the other entitled *Canada Online! Year Two Report, 2007*,[5] mainly concerned parents' perceptions of their children's Internet use. In 2004, parents reported that 70 per cent of young people aged six to eleven spent around 2.8 hours online per week. Among those aged twelve to seventeen, 95 per cent spent an average of 8.8 hours online per week. When the survey was repeated in 2007, over 96 per cent of people aged twelve to seventeen spent more than 11.9 hours per week on the Internet.[6]

These studies also revealed changes in the level of trust parents had with respect to Internet security. For example, in 2004, 69 per cent of parents with children aged twelve to seventeen believed their children could browse the Internet safely. In 2007, that number had risen to 74 per cent. In 2009, the Centre francophone d'informatisation des organisations (CEFRIO, Centre Facilitating Research and Innovation in Organizations with Information and Communication Technology) undertook a study on new technology use habits, but mainly targeted twelve to twenty-four year olds.[7] In its report, CEFRIO found that young Quebecers aged twelve to seventeen spent around sixteen hours a week on the Internet.

In contrast with traditional media, access to, and content on, the Internet is not officially regulated or monitored by any authority in Canada. The virtually untrammelled accessibility to new media has nonetheless led government bodies and other parties to study whether and how to apply broadcasting and telecommunications laws to Internet content. The issue of any form of national regulatory intervention of course raises debate. Leaving aside the contentious issues associated with freedom of expression, the Internet is an international medium for content that transcends national borders, but there is no realistic prospect of enforcement other than at the national level. Moreover, it is estimated that over 2.26 billion people use the Internet,[8] which makes it much more difficult to identify users who engage in harmful acts.

Despite these difficulties, which result mainly from the globalization of the Internet, a number of countries, including Canada, are conscious of the need for regulatory intervention to limit access to certain content that is offensive or inappropriate for sensitive audiences, such as children. Some measures designed to improve Internet governance have thus been established in the form of standards, principles, and rules that vary from one jurisdiction to another. In this section, we will examine the evolution of the approaches taken by the various stakeholders in Canada.

8

The History of the Regulation of the Internet

ACTIONS TAKEN BY THE CRTC

With the growth in Internet use in Canadian homes in the 1990s, the Canadian government had to focus on the question of regulation. In 1999, the CRTC held public consultations on the communication and information services generally referred to as new media in connection with the Broadcasting Act and the Telecommunications Act. The purpose was to determine whether new media services constituted broadcasting and, as a consequence of that determination, whether the provisions of the Broadcasting Act would or would not apply.

Following the public consultations, the CRTC stated: "The majority of services now available on the Internet consist predominantly of alphanumeric text, and, therefore, do not fall within the scope of the Broadcasting Act and are thus outside the Commission's jurisdiction."[1] While the CRTC decided not to use the Broadcasting Act to regulate new media, it found that Canadian legislation combined with self-regulatory measures such as blocking tools were an efficient way to counter the publication of illegal and offensive content. In addition, the CRTC explained that its exemption order was intended to encourage stakeholders to employ the Internet's new potential and thus to favour innovation.

However, the CRTC was nonetheless fully aware that there is potentially offensive and illegal content on the Internet. The commission encouraged Internet service providers and the various industry associations, in coordination with government and other bodies, to work together, as they had in the past, to develop codes of conduct and other tools to fight against and prevent publication of offensive material, including "establishing complaint lines and industry ombudsmen as well as developing international arrangements. Such arrangements could include co-operation between law enforcement agencies for providing notice and take down of web sites disseminating such content."[2] The formal exemption order was consecrated in a public notice issued seven months later.[3]

THE FUTURE ENVIRONMENT FACING THE CANADIAN BROADCASTING SYSTEM

In December 2006, at the request of Cabinet (i.e., the Governor in Council) pursuant to its authority under section 15 of the Broadcasting Act, the CRTC undertook a report on the changing environment of the Canadian broadcasting system. The report, ultimately entitled *The Future Environment Facing the Canadian Broadcasting System*, identified the principal trends and technological changes developing in the Canadian broadcasting system. In particular, it showed how access to various media content had changed in a context in which over 93 per cent of households had access to the Internet and 48 per cent had high-speed service. Moreover, the report cited statistics that showed growing Internet consumption by young Canadians. In 2006, twelve to fourteen year olds spent 21 per cent of their time on the Internet, while fifteen to nineteen year olds spent 22 per cent. From 2003 to 2006, downloading of television shows from the Internet also rose from 6 to 9 per cent in the case of twelve to fourteen year olds, and from 10 to 19 per cent among fifteen to nineteen year olds.

PERSPECTIVES ON CANADIAN BROADCASTING IN NEW MEDIA

In 2008, the CRTC released *Perspectives on Canadian Broadcasting in New Media* in the framework of the New Media Project Initiative. The purpose of the report was "to examine the cultural, economic, and technological issues associated with new media broadcasting."[4] The CRTC painted a picture of the changing new media environment, and to justify the study it invoked the constant evolution in the industry in recent years:

- High-speed residential Internet access is now available to 93% of households across the country and has been adopted by more than 60% of Canadian households.
- Consumers have adopted a wide array of Internet-connected and multimedia-capable devices (fixed and mobile) available at steadily declining prices and with functionality and features that continue to increase.
- Canadians are spending more time accessing broadcasting content over the Internet and on mobile devices and are asserting greater control while doing so.
- Technologies that enable the delivery of high quality broadcasting content on new media platforms are in commercial use.
- Globally, the pace at which professionally produced broadcasting content is being made available online is accelerating, but Canadian participation is lagging with respect to the amount of high quality, professionally-produced new media broadcasting content available and the level of early stage investment in the new media broadcasting environment.
- Advertisers are increasingly embracing new media broadcasting marketing strategies. Internet advertising expenditures, of which new media broadcasting is expected to garner an increasingly greater share, continue to grow at unsurpassed rates.[5]

Moreover, the report targeted the primary changes and orientations to be adopted to improve the new media environment:

- the need for increased support for Canadian new media broadcasting content;
- the need to promote Canadian content in a global new media broadcasting environment;
- the need to study the impact of traffic management techniques on new media broadcasting insofar as they may impair access to Canadian content; and
- the need for clearer definitions concerning new media broadcasting.[6]

Given the rapid evolution of technologies that support new broadcasting media, the CRTC found it imperative to assess the possibility of amending certain norms and legislation that applied to the Internet.

BROADCASTING REGULATORY POLICY CRTC 2009-329

In 2009, after more than five public consultations and a number of research reports on the evolution of regulations, computer technology, and new media, as well as diversification of Internet content, the CRTC renewed its 1999 order to better accommodate the rapidly changing new media landscape in Review of Broadcasting in New Media.[7]

In 2009, the CRTC decided to maintain the exemption status of new media broadcasting undertakings.[8] The Broadcasting Act would not apply to Internet content, as the new technology was still changing in a way that continued to justify various exemptions. Then, in February 2011, the Supreme Court of Canada stated that Internet providers do not fall under the laws that apply to broadcasters since they have no control over the content they distribute. This decision settled the ongoing debate to determine whether or not Internet service providers were broadcasters.[9]

INDUSTRY CANADA'S CONTRIBUTIONS

Illegal and Offensive Content on the Internet

In 2000, after it published *Regulation of the Internet – A Technological Perspective* and the CRTC adopted recommendation 1999-197, Industry Canada published *Illegal and Offensive Content on the Internet*. The report was part of the initiative of both Connecting Canadians and the Canadian government's attempt to promote a safer technological environment. It tackled the question of illegal and offensive Internet content to which Canadians have access. It described the government's strategy for dealing with such content, and provided an overview of concerted action taken by the public and private sectors to provide Canadians with the tools they need to use the Internet in a careful, safe, and responsible manner. In particular, it tried to directly raise parents' awareness of content that might not be appropriate for their children. The report noted that such content is mainly available on commercial and personal websites, on UseNet forums, in discussion groups, and in advertising.

In the report, the government indicated it would take action along five lines:

- supporting initiatives that educate and empower users;
- promoting effective use of industry self-regulation;
- strengthening the enforcement of laws in cyberspace;
- implementing hotlines and complaint reporting systems; and
- fostering consultation between the public and private sectors, and their counterparts in other countries.[10]

The report thus recommended that parents more closely supervise their children's online activities. At the same time, it encouraged parents to adopt certain attitudes towards those activities. It described a number of tools designed to prevent young people from access to illegal and offensive content, by raising their awareness of both the dangers in material available on the Internet and also recourse to relevant help lines and regulatory websites.

Cyberbullying

Canadian authorities have recently begun to focus on cyberbullying. While bullying has been an issue for some time, the adoption of technology and social media by children and teenagers has resulted in a greater prevalence of cyberbullying and related problems. In 2009, a survey by Statistics Canada revealed that 9 per cent of children between the ages of eight and sixteen have been victims of cyberbullying. It also found that girls and children between the ages of twelve and thirteen are more at risk of becoming victims than other children.[11] In December 2011, the Standing Senate Committee on Human Rights announced its intention to conduct an in-depth study on the phenomenon.[12] It heard testimonials and gathered information on cyberbullying and, at the end of 2012, released its report *Cyberbullying Hurts: Respect for Rights in the Digital Age*, which included recommendations to the government on how to react to this situation and how to help children handle victimization in all its forms.[13]

Resolution on Children's Online Privacy

On another level, as children have become frequent Internet users, the Office of the Privacy Commissioner of Canada issued a statement of Canada's privacy commissioners and privacy oversight officials in which it registered its commitment to promoting and raising awareness of online child privacy (a similar initiative was undertaken by the Quebec government).[14] The action it will take includes producing material and holding awareness campaigns to inform children and teenagers about the issues that surround new technologies. The privacy commissioner has also developed the Resolution on Children's Privacy Online, which calls on the industry, government, and other service providers to prioritize children's online privacy.[15] The commissioner's actions will be mostly educational, and will take the form of providing information to the public and releasing recommendations to the industry on best practices.[16]

Regulating Content on the Internet: A New Technological Perspective

In 2008, Industry Canada ordered an update of its 1999 publication *Regulation of the Internet – A Technological Perspective*. The new report, *Regulating Content on the Internet: A New Technological Perspective*, described the Internet's new features and trends that reflect the changing nature of media, the possibilities for regulation, and the limitations of restrictive technologies.

The new report pointed out the considerable increase in the number of Internet users, as well as the increase in the number of sources that create content. Indeed, it found that the number of web hosts had gone from around 100 million in 1999 to more than 500 million in 2007. Among other consequences of this growth, there were greater publication possibilities and a trend towards developing technologies to put a wide range of interactive audio and video content online. The report had three main conclusions:

- it is as impossible today as it was in 1999 to create a meaningful list of pre-identified content or content sources to be blocked or promoted;

- the costs of implementing a program to filter the volumes of data transiting the Internet based on a rule-set of any complexity would make it as prohibitively expensive as it was in 1999; and
- any regime that interfered with the fast and secure exchange of information over the Internet would have a negative effect on the competitiveness and profitability of Canadian businesses and on the Canadian economy.[17]

The report also discussed the evolution of various technologies for restricting access to certain content on the Internet, including the improved efficiency of tools to filter and target inappropriate content through the identification of IP addresses and geographical location. Despite advances, some difficulties with these tools remained:

- Development of new data encryption methods;
- Development of new protocol encryption methods;
- Development of new anonymous surfing software technologies;
- Deployment of new proxy sites;
- IP address flipping;
- DNS proxying; and
- Development of new data transfer protocols.[18]

Despite the numerous efforts to establish a general framework to protect children from inappropriate content on the Internet, the many reports mentioned above underscore the manifold technical constraints that limit any attempts to act on these questions.

APPLYING THE CRIMINAL CODE

Adoption of Bill C-15A

First introduced in the House of Commons in March 2001, Bill C-15A proposed "new Criminal Code provisions which seek to counter sexual exploitation of children involving the Internet."[19] The government introduced the bill following the Supreme Court's 2001 ruling in *R. v. Sharpe*, which established that the child pornography provisions in the Criminal Code were reasonable limitations on the right to freedom of expression provided for in section 2(b) of the Canadian Charter of Rights and Freedoms.[20] Bill C-15A, which was adopted in May 2002, amended section 163.1 of the Criminal Code to ensure that the prohibition concerning the production, distribution, and possession of child pornography extended to the Internet. In particular: "Clause 5(2) adds language to section 163.1(3) of the Code, which prohibits various acts of distribution of child pornography, to cover such things as 'transmission' and 'making available' in order to ensure that the offence extends to distribution of child pornography in electronic form on the Internet by such means as e-mail and posting items to websites."[21]

Moreover, the addition of section 172.1 to the code made it an offence "to communicate via a 'computer system' with a person under a certain age, or a person whom the accused believes to be under a certain age, for the purpose of facilitating the commission of certain sexual offences in relation to children or child abduction." This new section states that:

- the accused's belief in the victim's age may be inferred from a representation to the accused to that effect; and
- the accused is precluded from relying on the defence of mistake of fact as to the victim's age unless the accused took reasonable steps to ascertain the person's age.[22]

The foregoing modifications to the Criminal Code constitute a powerful step toward the establishment of strong measures to combat the sexual exploitation of children on the Internet.

The Canadian Strategy to Promote Safe, Wise and Responsible Internet Use, and Cybertip.ca

In February 2001, the government launched *Canadian Strategy to Promote Safe, Wise and Responsible Internet Use*.[23] Its purpose was to involve parents, teachers, and Internet service providers in protecting children from illegal content on, and sexual exploitation via, the Internet. The strategy aimed to:

- support initiatives that educate and empower users;
- promote effective industry self-regulation;

- strengthen the enforcement of laws in cyberspace;
- implement hotlines and complaint reporting systems; and
- foster consultation between the public and private sectors and their counterparts in other countries.[24]

In 2002, the government launched Cybertip.ca in collaboration with the Canadian Centre for Child Protection (CCCP) and other organizations from the public and private sectors, as well as non-profit groups. The public can use the site to report Internet content and issues such as:

- Child pornography (child abuse images and material)
- Online luring
- Child exploitation through prostitution
- Travelling to sexually exploit children
- Child trafficking[25]

Each month, Cybertip.ca receives around 700 reports of violations of the Criminal Code, all of which it forwards to the police for investigation. Cybertip.ca also sets up a number of initiatives every year to raise people's awareness of the dangers of the Internet and risks associated with other types of new technologies, such as smart phones.

Recommendations from the RCMP

The Royal Canadian Mounted Police (RCMP) has made recommendations concerning the Internet in a document entitled *Internet Security*. The document acknowledges that, though adults and children generally face similar risks, children are nonetheless more vulnerable. In particular, children face two types of risks:

- Risks related to individuals: "There are many ways to lure minors through the Internet. More particularly in chat rooms, nothing is easier than to pretend to be someone else. Some people take advantage of the relative anonymity offered by the Net to lie about their age, sex, occupation and ... intentions. For instance, sexual predators and pedophiles regularly participate in chat room discussions to find their victims. Ripoff artists are also very common."

- Risks related to offensive or inappropriate content: It is primordial to take measures to protect children.[26]

The RCMP provides a list of recommendations to inform parents of ways to minimize their children's exposure to such risks:

- You should always supervise your children as they surf the Net. Protection software is available that filters and blocks access to offensive sites. Browsers also offer some protection functions.
- Install the computer in a room shared by all family members like the living room.
- When you are not there, consider using a password to restrict access to the Internet. This allows for a better control by parents as they can monitor the activities of their children, especially if they are very young.
- Identify specific periods of time during the day when your children are allowed to use the computer, and set a time limitation on their surfing sessions.
- Ask yourself whether a child should take part in chat room discussions and use a Web cam.
- Take time to discuss with your children the dangers associated with the Internet, stressing the risks involved in chat rooms. Set security rules (for instance, not to open attachments, never give personal information to anyone, etc.).
- Take time to surf the Net with your children and to find out what they like!
- If your child is victim of luring, make sure not to delete the contact or the conversations. Isolate the computer and call your local police service. It is important for the investigators to have access to all the information.[27]

The RCMP also provides advice for children about how to use the Internet in an informed, safe manner:

1 Unless you have your parents' or a teacher's permission:
Never give out your name, address, phone number or the name of your school on the Internet;
Never send your photo;

Never give out your e-mail address or your password;
Never give out information concerning your parents.

2 If you feel in danger or uncomfortable on a chat, e-mail or web site, log off the Internet right away and tell your parents or a teacher about it.

3 Never arrange a meeting with an acquaintance made on the Internet unless one of your parents will be present.

4 When participating in chats, newsgroups and forums, always use a nickname that does not reveal anything about you.

5 Never open e-mails, links, pictures or games if you do not know the source. If in doubt, ask an adult first.

6 Never make a purchase online without your parents' permission.[28]

The RCMP defines child pornography as obscene or inappropriate material, and refers to section 163.1 of the Criminal Code of Canada, which defines such pornography as:

(a) a photographic, film, video or other visual representation, whether or not it was made by electronic or mechanical means,

(i) that shows a person who is or is depicted as being under the age of eighteen years and is engaged in or is depicted as engaged in explicit sexual activity, or

(ii) the dominant characteristic of which is the depiction, for a sexual purpose, of a sexual organ or the anal region of a person under the age of eighteen years;

(b) any written material, visual representation or audio recording that advocates or counsels sexual activity with a person under the age of eighteen years that would be an offence under this Act;

(c) any written material whose dominant characteristic is the description, for a sexual purpose, of sexual activity with a person under the age of eighteen years that would be an offence under this Act; or

(d) any audio recording that has as its dominant characteristic the description, presentation or representation, for a sexual purpose, of sexual activity with a person under the age of eighteen years that would be an offence under this Act.

The RCMP makes it clear that production and possession of child pornography are both crimes.

SELF-REGULATION OF INTERNET CONTENT

So far, there has been little official regulation of Internet content for children. However, when the Internet began to spread, the industry amended a number of self-regulatory codes to deal with online content in ways similar to that of other traditional media. Rather than having government authorities impose rules on them, companies preferred to regulate themselves. Even then, self-regulation is sometimes difficult to enforce and may thus have only a limited impact.

Advertising to Children in Canada: A Reference Guide

The 2006 version of *Advertising to Children in Canada: A Reference Guide*[29] encourages the development of responsible advertising from a self-regulatory perspective in all media, and so acknowledges the importance of the Internet in the lives of children and adolescents. The guide was produced by the CAB, the ASC, the ACA, the CCA, and the ICA.

The Canadian Marketing Association's Code of Ethics and Standards of Practice says that the directives concerning marketing to children and adolescents in chapter 5 of its Code of Ethics and Standards of Practice apply to all media, including those online.[30]

The Canadian Association of Internet Providers' Initiatives

In 2002, the Canadian Association of Internet Providers (CAIP) issued *Supporting the Government of Canada's "Strategy on Illegal and Offensive Content on the Internet: Promoting Safe, Wise and Responsible Internet Use."*[31] In the brochure, CAIP encourages its members to act in ways consistent with the behaviour and objectives it promotes. The purpose of the guide is to raise CAIP members' awareness of the need to study complaints about illegal content on the Internet. CAIP's involvement in preventing access to illegal and offensive content on the Internet is not new. In support of the Canadian government's publication of *Illegal and Offensive Content on the Internet*,[32] CAIP established a number of initiatives:

- Supporting Initiatives that Educate and Empower Users (this includes information provided to customers [online, ads, newsletters, billing inserts, welcome sheets, etc.] which alert them to the potential pitfalls of the Internet and advise them on how to protect themselves and their families; support for Internet educational organizations such as the Media Awareness Network, local libraries and schools; and research undertaken that is made publicly available) ...
- Promoting Effective Self-Regulation (this includes Acceptable Use Policies; provisions for resolving complaints and other initiatives, such as internal codes, in addition to adhering to CAIP's Code of Conduct; offering, supporting or providing information about technological or other tools such as child-friendly search engines and web sites, user or ISP-based filtering services, content-labeling services like ICRA, family web user agreements or rules, etc.) ...
- Strengthening the Enforcement of Laws in Cyberspace (this includes formal or informal working relationships with local police offices, provincial police or the RCMP; training for law enforcement; staff assigned to or even dedicated to dealing with law enforcement issues and officers; policies for dealing with potentially illegal content and handling related complaints and police investigations; support – whether direct or in-kind – for organizations dealing with law enforcement or related issues).
- Implementing Hotlines and Complaint Reporting Facilities (this includes individual hotline initiatives in addition to support for the Canadian hotline study, forums for accepting customer complaints and support for other anti-crime initiatives such as Crime Stoppers, etc.) ...
- Fostering Consultation between the Public and Private Sectors, and their Counterparts in other Countries (this includes membership or participation in international organizations, forums, conferences examining and addressing Internet content issues, collaboration with affiliates or parent companies in other countries).[33]

In a demonstration of initiative – though one now dated and not currently applicable – CAIP published its *CAIP's Internet Tips for Parents*[34] and *CAIP's Children's Online Pledge*, a series of commitments for children who use a computer to access the Internet that CAIP recommended be filled in and posted adjacent to the monitor.[35] CAIP has also published its own Code of Conduct, which is currently in effect.[36]

Collaboration by the Canadian Centre for Child Protection

The CCCP (protectchildren.ca) is dedicated to the personal safety of all children and works in collaboration with the Canadian government. It tries to prevent violence to children through two separate programs designed to raise awareness of the dangers children face on the Internet.

Its first program, Kids in the Know, is designed to raise the awareness of teachers, families, and children in order to strengthen young people's personal safety and to protect them against sexual exploitation and other dangers on the Internet. On its website (www.kidsintheknow.ca), Kids in the Know publishes a number of pages and educational guides on the primary dangers children face online, such as sexual predators.

The second program is found on Cybertip.ca (discussed above), which was developed in collaboration with the Canadian government.

OTHER STAKEHOLDERS

A number of interest, research, and other groups have stakes in regulating content for and ensuring the well-being of young people. While it would be difficult to provide an exhaustive list of such organizations, the following groups have been among the most active for a number of years and address both traditional and new media.

MediaSmarts

MediaSmarts (mediasmarts.ca), formerly the Media Awareness Network, is a Canadian not-for-profit charitable organization for digital and media literacy. Created in 1996, this organization provides access to a wide collection of educational resources on media and new technologies that parents, teachers, researchers, and youth can use to better understand the world of media and its influence. For instance, in addition to its own extensive website (www. mediasmarts.ca), MediaSmarts runs a comprehensive Internet safety website for parents (www.bewebaware.ca), which helps parents better understand what kids do online and offers guidelines to address any challenges that may arise.

MediaSmarts also conducts one of the most comprehensive and wide-ranging ongoing studies of children and teens' Internet use in Canada: *Young Canadians in a Wired World*.[37] Phases one and two of this ongoing research project – which were funded by the Canadian government and which tracked and investigated the behaviours, attitudes, and opinions of Canadian children, youth, and parents – were conducted between 2000 and 2005. These phases included focus groups with parents and youth, interviews with 1,081 parents and surveys of close to 11,000 students ages nine to seventeen. The research has raised a number of issues that demand society's attention and, more importantly, has highlighted the importance of education as a key response in helping young people make smart and informed online decisions and take advantage of the incredible opportunities offered by new media.

Phase two of the *Young Canadians in a Wired World* study revealed Internet access is almost universal among young people in Canada. More than half of respondents (61 per cent) said they had access to high-speed Internet at home. One third (33 per cent) of young people in Grade 8 said that they downloaded films and television shows online.

The current phase of the study began in 2010, with funding from the Office of the Privacy Commissioner of Canada and the Canadian Internet Registration Authority.[38] Its first qualitative findings were released in early 2012 in *Young Canadians in a Wired World: Teachers' Perspectives*.[39] This report is based on interviews with a purposive sample of ten teachers across Canada. The teachers interviewed agreed that children are expert users of new technologies but, for technology to be relevant in the classroom, need to be accompanied as they discover them as a learning tool. The interviewees reported that the then-new smartphone and tablet technologies can be useful educational tools, as they can adapt easily to fit each student's needs. Teachers then facilitate and optimize students' learning experience through the use of new technology. At the same time, the interviewees stressed the need to educate children about the importance of respectful and responsible online behaviour. The latest qualitative findings of the

Phase three series, *Talking to Youth and Parents about Life Online*, a national survey of 5,500 students in Grades 4 to 11 that began in 2011, were released in 2012.[40]

The Youth Media Alliance

The Youth Media Alliance (YMA) formed in 1974 as the Children's Broadcast Institute, which brought together representatives from the private and public sectors, business associations, broadcasters, media, advertising agencies, toy manufacturers, and other groups. In 1992, it renamed itself the Alliance for Children and Television. Today, its members are predominantly broadcasters, producers, and creators, and in 2010, in order to take into account the changes in the media world, it expanded its base and became the YMA. In a context in which content is increasingly deployed on new platforms, the new name better reflects the organization's current mission, which is to improve the quality of on-screen content for children and adolescents in Canada. The YMA pursues its goals through promotional activities, recognition, research, and training. In short, its objectives are to:

- provide professionals with ongoing training to help them meet the specific needs of children and teens;
- encourage high-quality content by rewarding Canada's best productions;
- make sure that the largest possible number of Canadian children and teens can regularly access high-quality content.[41]

With the backing of Bell Media, the YMA supported an exhaustive three-year, two-part study. Its first report, *A National Study on Children's Television Programming in Canada*, was published in 2010,[42] and its second, *Are the Kids All Right? Canadian Families and Television in the Digital Age*, was published in 2012.

The Centre for Youth and Media Studies

The Centre for Youth and Media Studies/Groupe de recherche sur les jeunes et les médias (CYMS) was officially inaugurated in February 1988, in the Department of Communications at the Université de

Montréal (www.grjm.umontreal.ca). The centre initially focused its research on analyzing television programming and viewing, promoting quality of content offered to young Canadian television viewers, and investigating the impact of such technologies on society. More recently, the CYMS has conducted research specifically on the psychosocial and cultural changes that result from the spread of emerging information and communications technologies.

The CYMS has conducted ground-breaking research in collaboration with Bell Media, Bell University Labs, the National Film Board, Quebec's Régie du cinéma, the Société des arts technologiques, the Montreal Science Centre, the Media Awareness Network, and the YMA. The CYMS remains the only bilingual Canadian university research centre with these objectives.

AN INTERNATIONAL LOOK

A number of studies and reports confirm that, in a great number of countries, children and teenagers have enthusiastically embraced the Internet and related technologies. In many of these countries, discussions have led to the creation of concrete legislation, regulation, and self-regulation of online safety measures for children. Each country where committees or commissions have investigated the Internet has a unique approach to the issue, and many are still developing applicable regulations.

In Canada, legislators are constantly revising the regulation of new media to cope with the fast-developing environment inherent to new technologies. It is therefore relevant to discuss what is happening in other areas of the world, though it is beyond our scope in this chapter to investigate them all. Instead, in the following sections we will concentrate on the European Union, the United Kingdom, the United States, and Australia – jurisdictions that, through their innovative efforts, have become leaders with respect to new media and its effects on children.

Europe

In recent years, Internet use has grown exponentially among younger people. Their use of new technology is widespread and integrated into their daily lives. A recent study by EU Kids Online used a sample of over 25,000 children between ages nine and sixteen from European countries to create a comprehensive portrait of how children use technologies.[43]

Most children access the Internet from home more often than from school, and most of them use a personal computer shared by the family; however, about 35 per cent of children have their own computer and can access the Internet from their bedroom. About a third of young people can access the Internet from a mobile device. Children go online mainly to get information for schoolwork, play games, watch video clips, and access social networking sites. According to a recent Swedish study, the average age of first contact with the Internet fell from thirteen to four between 2000 and 2009.[44]

These studies also conclude that children between the ages of nine and sixteen who use the Internet frequently face higher risks than those who access it infrequently. These children are at even greater risk of encountering strangers or viewing inappropriate content. Different studies underline that parents are rarely aware of this situation. Interestingly, a report on family and technology funded by the European Community suggests that parents are more predisposed to act as mediators for television than for Internet activities, even though they may be more concerned with the latter.[45] The report suggests that this is mostly due to a lack of skills on the part of parents. In addition, several other reports have shown that children perceive themselves as more skilled with technology than their parents, a perception that is particularly true for teenagers. A recent report made by Insafe (www.saferinternet.org), a European Union agency, underlines the fact that 70 per cent of children aged thirteen to fourteen have accounts on social networking sites, as do 80 per cent of those aged fifteen to sixteen.[46] The report also states that a high number of children under age thirteen are present on social networking sites, such as Facebook and MySpace, despite the fact that they are theoretically forbidden from accessing these sites. As the authors of these studies underlined, even if children risk harm online, they also encounter new opportunities. Therefore, discussions around what children do online should also be oriented towards the quality of the content they access.

The European Commission has worked to ensure that general legislation that includes the protection of children regulates the Internet. In 1998, the first legal document produced by the European

Union to take minors and the online environment into account was a list of recommendations designed to foster the protection of minors and human dignity in audiovisual and information services. The discussions by the Council of Europe led to a set of recommendations for member states and other concerned parties that included:

- promoting the voluntary establishment of national frameworks for the protection of minors and human dignity. This involves encouraging the participation of relevant parties (users, consumers, businesses and public authorities) in establishing, implementing and evaluating national measures taken in this domain. The establishment of a national framework for self-regulation of operators of on-line services is also encouraged;
- encouraging broadcasters to experiment, on a voluntary basis, with new ways to protect minors and inform viewers;
- fighting against illegal content on on-line services which causes offence to human dignity, by handling complaints and transmitting the necessary information about alleged illegal content to the relevant national authorities. Transnational cooperation between the complaints-handling structures is also encouraged in order to strengthen the effectiveness of national measures;
- promoting action to enable minors to make responsible use of on-line audiovisual and information services, notably by improving the level of awareness among parents, educators and teachers of the potential of the new services and of the ways in which they can be made safe for minors.[47]

At another Council of Europe meeting in 2006, these recommendations were updated to include new advances in technology and the proliferation of different media.[48] In the same vein, the European Commission adopted the Audiovisual Media Services Directives, a set of specific rules that aim to protect children from harmful content in any media, including the Internet. The general principles of this agreement entailed that all audiovisual media services should take action to comply with requirements in the following areas:

- identification of media service providers,
- prohibition of incitement to hatred,
- accessibility for people with disabilities,

- qualitative requirements for commercial communications,
- sponsoring, and
- product placement.[49]

In the early 2000s, member states of the European Community signed a convention designed to facilitate international cooperation in the fight against cybercrime.[50] In 2007, the European Community updated the convention to strengthen cooperation specifically with respect to online child sexual abuse material.[51] A bit earlier, in 2004, the European Council issued a framework[52] asking its member states to revise their definition of offences related to child pornography and ensure they had appropriate sanctions against all production, distribution, dissemination, transmission, acquisition, or possession of child pornography. That framework was revised in 2009 and led to the Council Framework Decision on Combating the Sexual Abuse, Sexual Exploitation of Children and Child Pornography.[53]

It is not possible for legislation to cover all of the content and risk of harm a child might face when navigating the Internet. That is why in 1999, parallel to these actions, the European Commission and its twenty-seven members created the Safer Internet Program, another major attempt to make the Internet safer for children.[54] The program was the result of a decision by the European Parliament and the European Council to adopt an action plan promoting safer Internet use. The Safer Internet Program's first phase was intended to span 1999 to 2004; it was then renewed for 2004 to 2009; and is now in its third phase, from 2009 to 2013.[55] This last phase of the Safer Internet Program also has a specific focus on cyberbullying. Indeed, the program will fund studies on this matter along with several initiatives to help parents and young people face this issue.

In general, the main focuses of the Safer Internet Program are:

- Fighting illegal content
- Tackling harmful content
- Promoting a safer environment
- Raising awareness[56]

The program aims to encourage different stakeholders to pursue these objectives. Additionally, it funds the different agencies that work towards them. The agencies are involved in giving educational information to parents and children about potentially harmful behaviour and how to behave safely online. The agencies also raise awareness about illegal content and how to report it. To pursue this objective, the centres, which we discuss below, have established INHOPE (www.inhope.org), a hotline through which people can easily report illegal content they have found on the Internet. Thus, the Safer Internet Program and its different agencies provide guidelines and recommendations and encourage companies and Internet providers to follow them, but do not have the authority to impose sanctions.[57]

SAFER INTERNET CENTRES Under these programs, the European Union has developed the Safer Internet Centres, which are part of Insafe (www.saferinternet.org), an organization that works to develop information on and awareness of safer Internet practices. The centres are present in thirty European countries and often organize information sessions to teach children, parents, and teachers about children's safety online. The centres also consult youth panels when developing their information material. In addition, they organize Safer Internet Day annually to raise awareness, and convene different parties involved in the program, such as Internet content providers. This yearly meeting has lead to two agreements on self-regulation: one on mobile phones and another on social networking sites.[58]

MOBILE TECHNOLOGIES In February 2007, the mobile industry, including content providers and major mobile operators, signed the *European Framework for Safer Mobile Use by Younger Teenagers and Children*, which aims to develop online techniques so children and teenagers can safely access the Internet from their mobile devices.[59] According to reports from GSMA Europe,[60] the ninety-one companies that have signed the agreement are currently implementing the measures they agreed to.[61] Consequently, these self-regulatory principles are present in twenty-five member states.

The framework's key recommendations for operators are:

- Classification of commercial content – mobile operators' own and third-party commercial content should be classified in line with existing national standards of decency and appropriateness so as to identify content unsuitable for viewing by children and younger teenagers;

- Access control mechanisms – appropriate means for parents for controlling children's access to this content should be provided;
- Education and awareness-raising – mobile operators should work to raise awareness and provide advice to parents on safer use of mobile services, and ensure customers have ready access to mechanisms for reporting safety concerns;
- Fighting illegal content on mobile services and the Internet – mobile operators should work with law enforcement agencies, national authorities and INHOPE or equivalent bodies to combat illegal content on the Internet.[62]

SOCIAL NETWORKING PRINCIPLES FOR THE EU Several social networking sites have agreed to self-regulate. Following a public consultation started by the Safer Internet Programme on child safety, eighteen companies agreed to follow a set of principles to ensure child safety when youngsters are using their websites. They also agreed to provide the European Commission with a declaration in which they explain how they apply these principles.[63] The principles are:

Principle 1: Raise awareness of safety education messages and acceptable use policies to users.
Principle 2: Work towards ensuring that services are age-appropriate for the intended audience.
Principle 3: Empower users through tools and technology.
Principle 4: Provide easy-to-use mechanisms to report conduct or content that violates the Terms of Service.
Principle 5: Respond to notifications of illegal content.[64]

OFCOM Among the European countries, the United Kingdom has made specific innovative efforts in regards to children and online safety. In this region, the regulatory authority on communication is the Office of Communication, known as Ofcom, a government body that fills a role equivalent to that of the CRTC in Canada.[65] It has regulatory authority over radio, television, and telecommunications.[66] When it comes to the Internet, Ofcom is the leading force in combating web content that is considered harmful or offensive, but its authority remains limited by the legal framework. It tackles children's online safety by encouraging stakeholders to adopt self-regulatory measures, mainly through mandatory codes of conduct.

One such code of conduct was established in 2004 for mobile operators and aims to control and classify some of the content available to children through mobile devices.[67] Despite the difficulty of controlling Internet content, commercial content providers' voluntary adoption of the classification framework made it possible for mobile operators to effectively block access to inappropriate content, thus protecting children from being exposed to it. The classification framework is intended to be broad enough to include most of the commercial content available in the United Kingdom. It states that if the content depicts nudity, sexual activity, offensive language, drugs, or graphic violence, commercial content providers must indicate that it should only be accessed by adults aged eighteen and over. Finally, it is worth mentioning that this attempt to control content access from mobile devices had great influence on implementation of the *European Framework for Safer Mobile Use by Younger Teenagers and Children*.[68]

ONLINE MARKETING In the United Kingdom, the advertising industry has adapted its codes of conduct to include the new media environment. In 1995, the Advertising Standards Authority (ASA) expanded to include "non-broadcast electronic media."[69] In 2010, the ASA extended its online authority to include those medias' "own marketing communications on their own websites and in other non-paid-for space under their control."[70] The Committee of Advertising Practice is responsible for the Code of Non-broadcast Advertising, Sales Promotion and Direct Marketing.[71] This code includes a specific section on advertising to children in which it calls on the advertising and marketing industry to consider children's specific characteristics when advertisements address them.[72]

OTHER STAKEHOLDERS Among other players involved in the protection of minors, the Internet Watch Foundation is a self-regulatory body reliant on European funding.[73] The mission of this organization is, on one hand, to help Internet service and content providers from the United Kingdom block sexually abusive content and, on the other hand, to facilitate easier ways to denounce such problematic web content. This organization works with the UK government to fight harmful online content and does so by encouraging Internet service and content providers to self-regulate. This self-regulatory effort reflects the best practices adopted by the industry, and members of the foundation can voluntary adopt this code of practice. The foundation's actions are concentrated in the United Kingdom, but it reaches an international level through its association with INHOPE.

The United States

As in Europe, different studies have tried to measure children's use of technology in the United States. A recent report produced by the Sesame Workshop explains that a significant number of young children – 25 per cent of three year olds and 50 per cent of five year olds – access the Internet daily.[74] Nonetheless, even if new technologies have become part of their daily activities, television remains the medium young children use most until age eight. Around that age, a shift in media consumption occurs as children begin to use more portable music players and video game consoles. A major trend observed in children's use of media is that they tend to multitask, using several media at the same time. For instance, children between ages twelve and seventeen often surf the web as they listen to music and use instant messaging to communicate with their friends.[75]

According to recent studies from the Pew Research Center's Internet and the American Life Project, 80 per cent of teens aged twelve to seventeen are active on social networks. According to a study by the Kaiser Family Foundation, children between ages eight and seventeen spend an average of seven hours a day consuming different media and, because they multitask, are actually exposed to ten hours of content. Moreover, the results from that study indicate that a growing number of children have access to media from their own rooms. An average of 71 and 33 per cent of children between ages eight and seventeen have access to a television or the Internet, respectively, in their bedrooms. The authors of the study underline that such migration of media to the bedroom could foster even higher consumption.[76]

In the United States, the Federal Communications Commission (FCC) is the legislative body that regulates interstate and international communications by radio, television, cable, satellite, and wire.[77] It has the authority to take action against pornography and violence, as well as harmful depiction of women and minorities in media; however, due to the difficulty inherent in regulating the Internet, it has limited authority over online content.

One of the first legislative attempts to protect children online was an act of Congress oriented towards criminalization of the transmission of indecent material to minors and of the display of offensive material. The 1996 Communication Decency Act (CDA), which is administered by the Federal Trade Commission, was designed to incriminate producers of such content and their Internet service providers.[78] This first attempt led to the major document on childhood online safety in 1998: the Children's Online Privacy Protection Act (COPPA).[79] COPPA regulates the information that website operators collect from children. It requires that operators and companies that provide online content comply with a set of provisions concerning collection and disclosure of information on users known to be under the age of thirteen. The principal rules for companies are:

- Post a clear and comprehensive privacy policy on their website describing their information practices for children's personal information;
- Provide direct notice to parents and obtain verifiable parental consent, with limited exceptions, before collecting personal information from children;
- Give parents the choice of consenting to the operator's collection and internal use of a child's information, but prohibiting the operator from disclosing that information to third parties;
- Provide parents access to their child's personal information to review and/or have the information deleted;
- Give parents the opportunity to prevent further use or online collection of a child's personal information;
- Maintain the confidentiality, security, and integrity of information they collect from children.[80]

In September 2011, due to the proliferation of different platforms and accessible information, an amendment to COPPA was proposed to limit the types of information that could be collected from children. The Do Not Track Kids Act of 2011 aimed to prohibit various websites and online operators "from: (1) using, disclosing to third parties, or compiling personal information collected from children or minors for targeted marketing purposes; and (2) collecting geolocation information in a manner that violates the regulations prescribed under this Act."[81]

A decade earlier, the Children's Online Internet Privacy Protection Act of 1998 became law.[82] Among other things, this act stated that in order to receive a portion of their government funding, primary and secondary schools and public libraries had to use Internet filters and other measures to protect children from potentially harmful content.[83]

The US government has also developed OnGuard Online (www.onguardonline.gov), a website dedicated to safety online that focuses mainly on child safety, as well as furnishing tips to parents and educators on how to advise children on potential harm and remaining safe online. It contains articles on different topics, such as how to avoid scams and delete cookies, as well as on cyberbullying, texting, and chatting, and gives parents tips on how to address these issues with their children.

COPPA AND SOCIAL NETWORKING SITES In a reaction to and in order to comply with COPPA, operators of social networking sites have decided to restrict access by children under age thirteen through terms of service agreements. A recent study by the University of Chicago found that, despite the law, many children have accounts on Facebook, the leading social networking site.[84] By the age of ten, 19 per cent of children already have accounts on Facebook, 32 per cent have accounts by age eleven, 55 per cent by age twelve, 69 per cent by age thirteen, and 78 per cent by age fourteen. The study also found that, among the parents interviewed, 63 per cent had helped their child set up an account and 89 per cent were aware their child had an account. This indicates that an age restriction does not eliminate the risk of young children logging onto social networking sites and being exposed to potential harm. To reduce this harm, the study proposes that social networks develop tools to enable parents to have better control over what their children have access to and what information they display.

ATTEMPTS TO CREATE WEBSITE CLASSIFICATION SYSTEMS Since the advent of the Internet, online content regulation has raised questions both about how to apply a degree of control and also about how to develop a classification system. Just as for television shows, films, and videos, such a system would allow consumers to block types of content that they might find offensive or inappropriate.

A number of online classification systems have been established to enable individuals to make choices according to specific criteria. In some cases, classification is based on the consumer's maturity, and in others, it is based on criteria specific to that system. The primary Internet sites and programs that have been developed are those of the Internet Content Rating Association (ICRA); although it no longer exists, it was an international non-profit organization based mainly in the United Kingdom and the United States. Its purpose was to protect children by establishing a safer online environment. The ICRA offered Internet content providers the means to classify their content through pre-approved rating by an international panel, and the resulting information allowed parents to filter the web sites their children could access. The ICRA is now incorporated into the Family Online Safety Institute (FOSI), which we will describe below.[85]

Other associations and private companies have also designed classification systems, but none of them have obtained legal status. Consequently, they are essentially preventive systems. This is the case of SafeSurf (www.safesurf.com), which introduced its first online classification system – named the SafeSurf Rating System in 1998 – in 1995. It is one of the most detailed classification tools available online. One of its special features is that it gives individuals some flexibility with respect to choice of filtering criteria. The system analyzes not only the description of the content on line, but also the way it is presented.

Another system developed in the United States, TRUSTe (www.truste.com), has provided advice concerning Internet privacy and security since 1997. It allows the public to submit complaints, which helps to keep its list of certified sites up to date. TRUSTe has certified over 3,500 websites, which makes it the biggest program of its type in the world.

In 1998, the Entertainment Software Rating Board (ESRB, www.esrb.org) launched Entertainment Software Rating Board Interactive (ESRBi), which classified and provided information about web sites and online games according to age appropriateness. ESRBi ceased operations in 2003, but ESRB maintained its Privacy Online Program, which it had established in 1999 and which was one of the first online classification programs to be approved by the Federal Trade Commission (FTC) in the framework of COPPA. This certification is proof of the tool's efficiency and quality with respect to protecting young people from offensive and illegal content on the Internet and keeping their identities safe. So far, more than 400 sites have received the ESRB Kids Privacy Certified rating.[86]

Though these classification systems are based in the United States, their use is voluntary and so Canadian operators and users can also employ them.

MOBILE TECHNOLOGY In November 2011, CTIA (www.ctia.org) and ESRB announced that six major mobile application providers would use a rating system based on existing computer and video game content classification systems. With the implementation of this system, the only existing one for the major applications, parents and users would be better informed about the maturity level of application content.[87]

ONLINE MARKETING The National Advertising Review Council (NARC) established the Children's Advertising Review Unit in 1979.[88] The unit is a self-regulatory program for industry stakeholders designed to ensure that advertising to children is appropriate. In 1996, the NARC revised the program to include guidelines about the new media environment and advertising online. The first core principle is now: "Advertisers have special responsibilities when advertising to children or collecting data from children online." The guidelines also now refer to specific topics related to advertising to children, such as material disclosure and contests, and have been adapted to include online advertisements. For example, the following relates to material disclosure and disclaimers:

> Advertisers that create or sponsor an area in cyberspace, either through an online service or a Website, must prominently identify the name of the sponsoring company and/or brand in that area. This could be done by using wording such as "Sponsored by ______."

While the following relates to sweepstakes and contests:

> Online contests or sweepstakes should not require the child to provide more information than is reasonably necessary. Any infor-

mation collection must meet the requirements of the Data Collection section of the Guidelines and the federal Children's Online Privacy Protection Act (COPPA).[89]

Moreover, a section on online sales has been added to the Children's Advertising Review Unit program. It contains the following guidelines:

- Advertisers who sell products and services to children online should clearly indicate to the children when they are being targeted for a sale.
- If an advertiser offers the opportunity to purchase any product or service, either through the use of a "click here to order" button or other on-screen means, the ordering instructions must clearly and prominently state that a child must have a parent's permission to order.
- Online advertisers must make reasonable efforts, in light of all available technologies, to provide the person responsible for paying for such products and services the means to exercise control over the transaction.
- If no reasonable means is provided to avoid unauthorized purchases by children online, the advertiser should enable the person responsible for payment to cancel the order and receive full credit without incurring any charges.[90]

In 2011, the FTC released two principles with which the marketing industry must comply. The first principle, "Meaningful Contribution to a Healthful Diet," aims to reduce advertising of unhealthy food to children, for example, the association of cartoon characters with food with high levels of fat or sugar. The second principle, "Nutrients with Negative Impact on Health or Weight," encourages the adoption of healthy food by children. These guidelines are particularly innovative because they include web-based and video game advertisements, which the FTC did not include in similar actions in the past. Even though the guidelines are not mandatory, the FTC strongly recommends compliance with them.[91]

OTHER STAKEHOLDERS Alongside industry and governmental efforts to regulate web content accessible to children, different independent groups have made it their mission to advocate children's online safety. Due to space constraints, we will discuss only a few.

FOSI (www.fosi.org) is an established leader in online safety. This non-profit organization works towards developing a safer Internet for children, and counts leading Internet service providers such as AOL, Yahoo, and AT&T among its members. FOSI's strategy aims to put children's online safety at the centre of its Internet regulation discussions. In order to achieve this objective, it provides Internet service providers and governments, mainly those of the United States and United Kingdom, with the latest informative research and comprehensive reports concerning media environments most pertinent to children and related online safety measures. It also organizes events and round table discussions at which stakeholders are invited to share their best practice strategies in order to make the Internet a safer environment for children and parents alike.

The American Association of Pediatrics (AAP) also discusses children and their Internet use. On its website (www.aap.org), articles offer families advice on how to keep an open dialogue about the Internet with their children. Further advice is presented though a collection of short videos from which parents can learn how to talk about social networking sites with their kids and how to set rules concerning Internet use.[92] However, though the AAP offers tips for Internet use, it groups the Internet with other media forms such as television and video games when making official recommendations. Thus, the general recommendation from the AAP regarding media is to limit children's exposure to screens, which includes time spent online.

The Center on Media and Child Health at Children's Hospital Boston, Harvard Medical School, and Harvard School of Public Health is another organization that promotes healthy media use (www.cmch.tv). The center focuses on academic research, and conducts, funds, and compiles projects that aim to foster a better understanding of the possible effects media may have on children's health and development. It also suggests articles with tips to help parents foster good Internet practices.

The National Association for Media Literacy Education (www.namle.net) has the exclusive mission to educate about safe media practices and works to give children and adults from all horizons a comprehensive understanding of all types of media and how they are appropriate. Among its many endeavours, it issues an electronic journal, the *Journal of Media Literacy Education*, in which it publishes recent research on media literacy.

Each of these groups tries to help and advise parents on their children's use of the Internet and other media platforms.

Australia

Like those around the world, Australian children have widely adopted technology in their daily routines. A study on a sample of about 400 children aged nine to sixteen confirms this trend, and found that 76 per cent of children surveyed access the Internet on a daily basis.[93] Moreover, statistics indicate that Australian children use the Internet more independently than Canadian children, with 46 per cent having access to the Internet from their bedrooms and 31 per cent from a mobile device. As in the rest of the world, in Australia, children have adopted social networking sites such as Facebook in large numbers and 65 per cent of children between nine and sixteen who have access to the Internet have accounts on such web sites. Not surprisingly, as in other countries, children under the age of thirteen also access these sites: 29 per cent of children aged nine to ten and 60 per cent of children aged eleven to twelve have accounts on social media sites.

The Australian Communications and Media Authority (ACMA), a federal agency, is responsible for all regulations concerning media, including the Internet. It was established in 2005 following the merger of the Australian Broadcasting Authority and the Australian Communications Authority.[94] With regards to Internet content regulation, the ACMA asks all Internet service providers to follow a code of conduct. Failure to do so is an offence under the Broadcasting Services Act (1992). On the self-regulatory side, the Internet Industry Association (IIA, iaa.net.au) issued the icode, a code of conduct that all Internet and mobile content providers must follow. The code prohibits specific types of Internet content that are considered harmful, namely, child pornography, bestiality, excessively violent material, and sexually violent material. The code also declares that content providers must ensure a safe Internet environment for all end consumers.[95]

Part of the icode directly advocates for online safety. It states that Internet and mobile content providers must ensure that parents are informed of good practices for when their children use the Internet. If Internet service providers comply with these principles, they may qualify as IIA Family Friendly Content Service Providers, which allows their websites to display the Online Safety Button, a direct link to a page that contains legal information regarding the sites themselves, tips for parents to help their children browse the Internet safely, and an explanation of how to submit complaints to ACMA.

Along with these joint efforts with the industry, ACMA has developed Cybersmart, a program to promote cybersafety and cybersecurity. Cybersmart is designed not only for children and teenagers, but also for parents and teachers. It aims to:

- Inform children, young people, parents, teachers and library staff about cybersafety issues
- Educate audiences through information, resources and practical advice
- Empower children and young people to be safe online.[96]

Cybersmart has taken different actions to fulfil these goals. The program funds the development of educational material that raises awareness on online safety. It funds the cybersafety contact centres, which parents can call to have more information about online safety, and it funds a helpline, which kids can call if they experience difficulties online. The program has also developed a comprehensive website that provides information about online safety to young children, children, teens, parents, and teachers.

OTHER STAKEHOLDERS Children's online safety is a concern shared not only by the government but also by members of the community. The Australian Council on Children and Media (ACCM) is a not-for-profit organization with a mission to develop children's awareness of the impact of media. To achieve this goal, the ACCM works on three different levels: educational, support, and research. It maintains an updated website (http://childrenandmedia.org.au) with information regarding recent developments on youth and media, issues a monthly digest, conveys this information to parents in a comprehensive way, and makes sure such information is accessible.

The organization supports the community with a helpline for parents and children's educators, which they can call if they face an issue related to children and media, as well as advice on taking action and how to make a complaint.[97] It offers reviews from a child's perspective on content directed at children, and though at this stage such reviews are only available for movies, the ACCM plans to extend them to television programs and video games. The ACCM also conducts research and funds projects that investigate children and media. When it comes to the Internet, the ACCM has a recent publication that explores different topics related to parents' potential questions about children's safety online. Some of the topics address the amount of time children should spend online, bedroom Internet access, and safe browsing.

CONCLUSIONS

New technologies are shaping young people's daily activities. As their use of new technologies has grown over the years, governments, the industry, and other stakeholders have come together to tackle the issues associated with online safety for children. The challenges of trying to apply and create regulations for the Internet rest mainly on its unsettled barriers, which go far beyond the scope of individual countries' legal frameworks. Yet, Internet regulations do exist and are now followed by the Internet industry's biggest stakeholders. Although our review of this topic cannot be completely exhaustive, the question of Internet regulation has become important on a global level.

Conclusion

The measures designed to regulate audiovisual content that targets children are based on mechanisms that control the environments in which such content circulates. These measures are necessarily neater and more effective in the case of broadcasting than in the case of the Internet. After all, there is a finite number of broadcasters in Canada, and each operates under a licence issued by the CRTC. In contrast, there is, relatively speaking, an infinite number of purveyors of content on the Internet, and they are unregulated and scattered across the globe. In that sense, there are no boundaries on the Internet in Canada, whether geographic or regulatory.

Where regulatory measures exist in broadcasting, they are often accompanied by preventive action plans designed to inform and educate the public about various kinds of effects. Such plans have come to be known as media literacy, and the importance of this educational approach to the resolution, indeed the avoidance, of content pitfalls has long been recognized. Consider, for example, the following statement, made as a part of the CRTC's violence policy of 1996: "The Commission's view ... continues to be that long-term public awareness and media literacy programs are paramount to changing attitudes about the acceptability of TV violence and to creating an understanding about the harmful effects of TV violence on children. The Commission also considers that, while industry codes, program classification and consumer-empowering technology will continue to play an essential role in addressing the issue, public awareness and media literacy programs represent most of the solution to TV violence."[1] In addition to the role that media literacy plays in the broadcasting area, where it accompanies other regulatory measures, it has a central role in the defence of children's interests on the Internet, where few if any proscriptions exist. The good news is that the opportunity to access literacy options are abundant for individuals, particularly parents, in their capacities as both television viewers and Internet surfers.

One user-controlled tool is the V-chip, which has been available on all North American television sets for a decade or so. Despite its prevalence, a 2007 survey undertaken by the Kaiser Family Foundation in the United States revealed that, though all televisions manufactured since 2000 contain V-chips, more than half the parents who had purchased a television set since that year were not aware that their set contained such a feature. Moreover, only one parent in six had ever used that program rating system.[2]

Despite the legislative initiatives in this area (whether enforced by governments or adopted by individuals in their own homes), it is unlikely that the public is sufficiently informed and ready to actively regulate the content to which children are exposed. The public's potential role is not negligible because it requires that viewers and users shoulder some of the social responsibility for the potential effects of heedless or careless watching and browsing. Responsibility for oversight cannot be left solely in the hands of regulatory or self-regulatory authorities.

The Netflix debate, which resulted from concerns raised by traditional broadcasters about what the CRTC and industry call *over-the-top programming services*, raises an interesting perspective regarding the issue of its hybrid, web-sourced, television-like programming. In popular understanding, Netflix, which streams movies and television episodes over the Internet to television monitors and other devices for a monthly fee, straddles the line between traditional broadcast and web content. For the time being, although traditional broadcasters have called upon the CRTC to impose a requirement for a minimum amount of Canadian content that the service must, as it understands matters, "broadcast," the CRTC has opted not to regulate it.[3] Even if the CRTC chooses not to address the regulatory challenge, as framed by the traditional broadcasters, the debate underscores the inevitable new challenges the CRTC and the public face in protecting children in the context of the regulation of content on the Internet and other more novel broadcasting services.

The regulatory controls designed to protect today's youth in the new online landscape are hardly set in stone. The CRTC has not yet developed a clear strategy related to the digital world of children. It is not certain whether the progressive, protective regulation and self-regulation in the areas of violence, stereotypes, and advertising that are now forcefully applied to traditional media can realistically be applied to new media. Indeed, it is a fair question whether the differences between the so-called traditional media and new media are as profound as they seem to be. Not even the authors of this book are entirely in agreement on this point.

In Canada, while there are legislative, regulatory, and self-regulatory rules that cover some aspects of the audiovisual and digital industry, there is room for the public to take some responsibility. Educated and involved parents are a realistic – and indeed an essential – complement to the regulatory tools required to address Canadians' viewing and using choices for the foreseeable future. That said, we are extremely sympathetic to the request of a number of CRTC chairs that Parliament add administrative monetary penalties to the commission's panoply of regulatory instruments, which will provide additional regulatory flexibility.

Looking at new media initiatives in other parts of the world, it appears that Canada could learn from others. First, the European Commission is a leading force behind the promotion of new media awareness. The Safer Internet Program provides support and information about online safety to parents and children, and brings important industry officials together to develop and implement new strategies. Through this program, the European Commission has encouraged the industry to adopt two innovative self-regulatory frameworks, one for mobile technologies and one for social networking sites – frameworks that still do not have a North American equivalent.

The United States' adoption of COPPA created well-defined rules concerning private information collected from children by online companies. This legislation provides the government a way to take legal action against offenders. To easily comply with this law, most websites restrict access to children over the age of thirteen, though younger children can overstep such restrictions through their physical invisibility to the operator. In any case, COPPA only deals with one aspect of the Internet dilemma, namely, the collection of user information, and does not address children's access to inappropriate content. Critics are not wrong when they argue that even this law does not adequately protect children from potential harm and that the emphasis should be put on giving parents the savvy and awareness they need to help their children navigate the Internet.

All these examples suggest that government and affiliated industry members must cooperate in order to establish adequate boundaries for the online content available to children. As we have demonstrated throughout this book, legislation can and does embody some government efforts, but it cannot hope to represent the whole solution to the protection of children. New media, both in broadcasting and online, will continue to require collaboration of the government, the industry, and the public. The full extent of the challenges that the unavoidably, unpredictably developing environment of new media is, as yet, unknowable. From this evolving perspective, we must attempt to regulate and self-regulate the spaces and worlds in which our children are growing up.

Notes

FOREWORD

1 Active Healthy Kids Canada, *Report Card on Physical Activity for Children and Youth*, May 2012.

2 Ipsos Reid, market research for MediaSmarts, 2005.

3 CRTC, "Environmental Scan of Digital Media Convergence Trends: Disruptive Innovation, Regulatory Opportunities and Challenges," 2011, http://www.crtc.gc.ca/eng/publications/reports/rp110929.htm.

INTRODUCTION

1 A first attempt to make such an inventory on Canadian regulation and self-regulation of audiovisual content for children was published some fifteen years ago and entitled *Systemized Summary of Canadian Regulations Concerning Children and the Audiovisual Industry*, by André H. Caron and Annie E. Jolicoeur (Montreal: Centre for Research in Public Law, Université de Montréal, 1996).

PART ONE

1 Statistics Canada, "Household Expenditures Research Series," 2010, CANSIM (62F0026M), table 203-0027.

2 BBM Canada, *BBM Canada Television Data 2011–2012*, BBM Canada: Toronto, 2012.

3 Television Bureau of Canada, *TV Basics 2010–2011*, http://www.tvb.ca/page_files/pdf/InfoCentre/TVBasics2010-2011.pdf.

CHAPTER ONE

1 The CRTC operates pursuant to the Canadian Radio-television and Telecommunications Commission Act, R.S.C., ch. C-22 (1985).
2 Broadcasting Act, S.C., ch. 11 (1991).
3 Ibid., s. 3(1)(b).
4 Ibid., s. 3(1)(c).
5 Ibid., s. 3(1)(d)(iii).
6 CRTC, Broadcasting Public Notice CRTC 1999-84, New Media, 17 May 1999.
7 CRTC, Broadcasting Notice of Public Hearing CRTC 2008-11, Notice of Consultation and Hearing, 15 October 2008.
8 CRTC, Broadcasting Regulatory Policy CRTC 2009-329, Review of Broadcasting in New Media, 4 June 2009.
9 Canadian Radio-television and Telecommunications Commission (Re), 2010 F.C.A. 178; Telecommunications Act, S.C., ch. 38 (1993).
10 *Reference re Broadcasting Act*, [2012] 1 S.C.R. 142.
11 The CRTC has hitherto sought, unsuccessfully, the broader availability of administrative monetary penalties as a part of its enforcement tools. See, for example, the CRTC's appearance before the Standing Committee on Canadian Heritage on 2 November 2010.
12 CRTC, Pay Television, Pay-per-View, Video-on-Demand and Speciality Services – Statistical and Financial Summaries 2004–2008, 2008.
13 CRTC, Broadcasting Public Notice CRTC 2003-10, Industry Code of Programming Standards and Practices Governing Pay, Pay-per-View and Video-on-Demand Services, 6 March 2003. This notice replaced the 1984 Pay Television Programming Standards and Practices, which became obsolete with the advent of pay-per-view television and video on demand.
14 CRTC, Broadcasting Regulatory Policy CRTC 2011-443, Standard Conditions of Licence, Expectations and Encouragements for Specialty and Pay Television Category A Services, 27 July 2011.

CHAPTER TWO

1 These events are described more fully in CIII-TV (Global Television) re "Mighty Morphin Power Rangers" (CBSC Decision 93/94-0270 and 93/94-0277), 24 October 1994. The new broadcaster code replaced the Violence Code originally established by the CAB in January 1987.

2 CRTC, Broadcasting Public Notice CRTC 1993-149, Voluntary Code regarding Violence in Television Programming, 28 October 1993.

3 CRTC, Broadcasting Public Notice CRTC 1993-99, Revised Broadcast Code for Advertising to Children, 30 June 1993.

4 Note, though, that the code does not apply to Quebec, where advertising directed at children has been prohibited since 1972 under the general regulation, as amended, made under the Consumer Protection Act (L.Q. 1971, c. 74).

5 According to section 32 of the Broadcasting Act, it is an offence for any person to carry on a broadcasting undertaking without holding a licence to do so.

6 CRTC, Broadcasting Decision CRTC 92-544, Le Réseau de Télévision TVA Inc, 13 August 1992.

7 CRTC, Broadcasting Decision CRTC 94-33, CTV Television Network Ltd, Television Network Licence Renewal, 9 February 1994.

8 CRTC, Broadcasting Public Notice CRTC 1999-97, Building on Success – A Policy Framework for Canadian Television, 11 June 1999, point 67.

9 CRTC, Broadcasting Decision CRTC 2000-2, Licences for CBC French-Language Television and Radio Renewed for a Seven-Year Term, 6 January 2000, s. 3.

10 Ibid., s. 45.

11 CRTC, Broadcasting Decision CRTC 2000-1, Licences for CBC English-Language Television and Radio Renewed for a Seven-Year Term, 6 January 2000, s. 57.

12 CRTC, "Types of TV Broadcasters," last modified 4 October 2009, http://www.crtc.gc.ca/eng/info_sht/b320.htm.

13 CRTC, Broadcasting Decision CRTC 2012-339, Saskatchewan Communications Network – Acquisition of Assets, 21 June 2012. SCN is no longer a stand-alone educational service; it is now a part of Rogers' CityTV network.

14 CRTC, Broadcasting Decision CRTC 2003-175, Licence Renewal and Additional Advertising for ACCESS, 6 June 2003.

15 CRTC, Broadcasting Decision CRTC 2009-444, CIVM-TV Montréal and Its Transmitters – Licence Renewal, 24 July 2009. Note: "The licensee requested that its network licence not be renewed because it will not be offering regional programming breakaways during its new licence term."

16 CRTC, Broadcasting Decision CRTC 2008-143, TFO – Licence Renewal, 16 July 2008.

17 Nordicity, *The Case for Kids Programming: Children's and Youth Audio-Visual Production in Canada*, 30 April 2009, 15.

18 CRTC, "Types of TV Broadcasters."
19 CRTC, Broadcasting Decision CRTC 2005-445, Aboriginal Peoples Television Network – Licence Renewal, 31 August 2005.
20 CRTC, Broadcasting Decision CRTC 2004-12, Teletoon/Télétoon Licence Renewal, 21 January 2004.
21 CRTC, Broadcasting Decision CRTC 2000-493, BBC Kids, 14 December 2000.
22 CRTC, Broadcasting Decision CRTC 2000-525, Discovery Kids, 14 December 2000.
23 CRTC, Broadcasting Decision CRTC 2008-257, YTV OneWorld – Category 2 Specialty Service, 18 September 2008.
24 CRTC, Broadcasting Decision CRTC 2002-386, Licence Renewal for Family, 28 November 2002.
25 CRTC, Broadcasting Decision CRTC 2006-381, YTV – Licence Renewal, 18 August 2006.
26 CRTC, Broadcasting Decision CRTC 2006-382, VRAK.TV – Licence Renewal, 18 August 2006.
27 Ibid.
28 CRTC, Broadcasting Decision CRTC 2004-27, Treehouse TV – Licence Renewal, 21 January 2004.
29 CRTC, Broadcasting Decision CRTC 2006-98, Vrak Junior – Category 2 Specialty Service, 27 March 2006.
30 CRTC, Broadcasting Decision CRTC 2010-103, TVA Junior – Category 2 Specialty Service, 22 February 2010.
31 The CBSC was the creation of *private* broadcasters and its direct authority does not currently encompass any public broadcasters. Public Notice CRTC 1991-90, 30 August 1991.
32 Pierre Trudel, "Les effets juridiques de l'autoréglementation," 1988–1989, 19 RDUS 247, 3. Our translation.
33 The precursor to that code dates back to 1943. A good number of the original standards remain in the code, which was most recently revised in 2002.
34 CAB, CAB Code of Ethics, 2002, http://www.cbsc.ca/english/codes/cabethics.php.
35 Actually, the CBSC only deals with Canada's private broadcasters; as a general rule, complaints that relate to the CBC and other public broadcasters are still (at the time of writing) dealt with by the CRTC.
36 In addition to the Code of Ethics, the CBSC administers six other codes, two of which we address in chapters 3 and 4.

37 CBSC, "The Special Role of the CBSC," http://www.cbsc.ca/english/about/role.php.

38 CBSC, "The CBSC's Structure," http://www.cbsc.ca/english/about/structure.php.

39 In one case involving the airing of a popular song, the CRTC asked the CBSC to undertake a national review of a regional decision, but the CRTC did not otherwise involve itself. See CHOZ-FM re the song "Money for Nothing" by Dire Straits (CBSC Review of Decision 09/10-0818), 17 May 2011.

40 Save three – two radio groups and one specialty service group, none of which has been a source of complaints to the CBSC or the CRTC – all significant broadcast groups in the country are CBSC members.

41 Radio broadcasters are not subject to the television Violence Code and conventional broadcasters are not subject to the pay television codes.

CHAPTER THREE

1 Canada, Office of the Co-ordinator, Status of Women, *Towards Equality for Women* (Ottawa: Supply and Services Canada, 1979).

2 Among other documents, see the task force's *Report on Self-regulation by the Broadcasting and Advertising Industries for the Elimination of Sex-Role Stereotyping in the Broadcast Media*, 1986.

3 CRTC, Broadcasting Public Notice CRTC 1986-351, 22 December 1986.

4 Pierre Trudel and France Abran, *Le droit de la radio et de la télévision* (Montreal: Éditions Thémis, 1991), 435.

5 Broadcasting Public Notice CRTC 1986-351.

6 CRTC, Broadcasting Public Notice CRTC 1990-99, Industry Guidelines for Sex-Role Portrayal, 26 October 1990, appendix A.

7 CRTC, Broadcasting Public Notice CRTC 1992-58, 1992 Policy on Gender Portrayal, 1 September 1992.

8 CRTC, Broadcasting Public Notice CRTC 1991-90, Canadian Broadcast Standards Council, 30 August 1991.

9 CBC, "Stereotypes in CBC/Radio-Canada Programming," in *Program Policies*, 21 September 2005.

10 Ibid.

11 Compare the CBC's policies and the concerns they express to the Equitable Portrayal Code as discussed below.

12 ASC, "Gender Portrayal Guidelines," Canadian Code of Advertising Standards, http://www.adstandards.com/en/Standards/genderPortrayalGuidelines.aspx.

13 CAB, CAB Code of Ethics, revised June 2002, http://www.cbsc.ca/english/codes/cabethics.php.

14 CBSC, Sex Role Portrayal Code for Television and Radio Programming, 26 October 1990, s. 4(d).

15 Ibid.

16 CRTC, Broadcasting Public Notice CRTC 1999-97, Building on Success – A Policy Framework for Canadian Television, 11 June 1999.

17 Ibid., s. 114. See s. 115–23 for further details and discussion.

18 Ibid., s.121.

19 CRTC, Broadcasting Public Notice CRTC 2001-88, Representation of Cultural Diversity on Television – Creation of an Industry/Community Task Force, 2 August 2001.

20 CAB, *The Presence, Portrayal and Participation of Persons with Disabilities in Television Programming*, 16 September 2005.

21 CRTC, Broadcasting Public Notice CRTC 2008-23, Equitable Portrayal Code, 17 March 2008.

22 All of the CBSC's decisions related to the Equitable Portrayal Code and all other broadcaster codes can be found at http://www.cbsc.ca/english/decisions/index.php.

CHAPTER FOUR

1 Royal Commission on Violence in the Communications Industry, *Report of the Royal Commission on Violence in the Communications Industry*, 50–1.

2 Ibid., 52.

3 Ibid., 53.

4 Two decades later, that crime remains unsolved.

5 Keith Spicer, *Life Sentences: Memoirs of an Incorrigible Canadian* (Toronto: McClelland & Stewart, 2004), 296.

6 CRTC, "CRTC Takes Proactive Approach to Addressing Television Violence," 27 May 1992.

7 Dave Atkinson and Marc Gourdeau, *Summary and Analysis of Various Studies on Violence and Television* (Ottawa: CRTC, 1991).

8 Andrea Martinez, *Scientific Knowledge about Television Violence* (Ottawa: CRTC, 1992).

9 CRTC, *Approaches to Violence in Television Programming*, July 1995, 13.

10 Ibid.

11 One of the two principal partners in AGVOT, the CCTA, disbanded in 2006.

Responsibility for administering all AGVOT-related information queries fell to the CBSC as of 1 March 2007. We will discuss AGVOT's activities related to the classification system and the V-chip later in this chapter.

12 The title of the code was originally the Voluntary Code regarding Violence in Television Programming, which was odd considering that the code was a *mandatory* condition of licence for every television broadcaster in Canada from 1 January 1994 on. Following a request by the CBSC's National Chair to the CRTC to eliminate confusion, the CRTC accepted the new simplified name, CAB Violence Code, as of 8 September 2008. We will use that title throughout this chapter.

13 CRTC, Broadcasting Public Notice CRTC 1993-149, Voluntary Code regarding Violence in Television Programming, 28 October 1993.

14 CBSC, CAB Violence Code, http://www.cbsc.ca/english/codes/violence.php #content.

15 The code defines *gratuitous* as "material which does not play an integral role in developing the plot, character or theme of the material as a whole."

16 CIII-TV (Global Television) re "Mighty Morphin Power Rangers" (CBSC Decision 93/94-0270 and 93/94-0277, 24 October 1994); see also the CBSC news release, "'Power Rangers' too Violent, Says Ontario Council," 1 November 1994.

17 CIII-TV (Global Television) re "Mighty Morphin Power Rangers."

18 Ibid.

19 Given the show's basic structural problems, the CBSC found it unlikely that those efforts could succeed. However, there were no further complaints or CBSC decisions in regards to that version of *Power Rangers*.

20 At the time, conventional broadcasters were the only CBSC members; specialty and pay television services only became eligible to join several years later.

21 The two broadcasters were YTV, which, although Canadian, was not then a member of the CBSC, and Fox, an American network not subject to Canadian programming rulings. The CBSC had no way of knowing that, on the release of the decision, YTV would immediately comply with the panel's conclusions.

22 CTV re Power Rangers Wild Force (CBSC Decision 02/03-0260), 2 May 2003.

23 Held pursuant to Notice of Public Hearing CRTC 1995-5, A Review of the Commission's Approach to Violence in Television Programming, 3 April 1995.

24 Ibid.

25 See "Possible Amendment to Cable Television Regulations, 1986," in Notice of Public Hearing CRTC 1995-5.

26 I.e., rather than the CBSC.

27 This point was an attempt to avoid the CBSC operational principle that only one complaint is necessary to open a file. In other words, for the CBSC, the complaint is justified or it is not. No threshold number of complaints changes the *quality* of the program.

28 Videotron, promotional brochure, 1994.

29 CRTC, "Chronology of Main Events and Initiatives Undertaken Related to the Issue of Television Violence," in CRTC, *Respecting Children: A Canadian Approach to Helping Families Deal with Television Violence* (1996), 6.

30 CRTC, Broadcasting Public Notice CRTC 1994-155, The Pay Television and Pay-per-View Programming Code regarding Violence, 21 December 1994. The services already had an Industry Code of Programming Standards and Practices Governing Pay, Pay-per-View, and Video-on-Demand Services.

31 CRTC, Broadcasting Public Notice CRTC 1995-5, Policy Governing the Distribution of Video Games Programming Services, 13 January 1995, conditions 6 and 7.

32 CBC, Program Policy No. 7, "Violence in Children's Programming," in CBC, Program Policies (6 July 1994) (now Program Policy No. 1.1.7).

33 CRTC, *Canada and TV Violence: Cooperation and Consensus* (1994). According to the CBSC's "Blocking Programs" (http://www.cbsc.ca/english/agvot/programs.php):

> The V-chip is a technology that allows television users to block out programming based on a rating system ... Invention of the V-chip is generally credited to Tim Collings while he was an engineering professor at Simon Fraser University in British Columbia, Canada. Other individuals, however, also claim to have invented similar technology ... Using the television set's on-screen menu, users can set the level of programming they wish to block. For example, if a user selects a PG rating, all programs at that level and below are allowed to pass through the V-chip and be viewed. Any programs with a rating above that level will be blocked and the screen will go blank.

34 CRTC, Broadcasting Public Notice CRTC 1996-36, Policy on Violence in Television Programming, 14 March 1996.

35 In the end, the CBSC never became involved in such a ratings clearinghouse function.

36 Broadcasting Public Notice CRTC 1996-36.

37 While Quebec-based broadcasters can use the Régie's ratings *structure*, they cannot apply the actual Régie *rating*; they are obliged to consider the rating level as a function of television broadcast, rather than one of cinema presentation. See TQS re The Movie L'Affaire Thomas Crown (The Thomas Crown Affair) (CBSC Decision 01/02-0622), 20 December 2002.

38 AGVOT, *A Review of the Commission's Approach to Violence in Television Programming*, Oral Presentation to the CRTC Hearing re: P.N. CRTC 1995-5, Hull, Quebec, 12 October 1995.

39 Telecommunications Act of 1996, Pub.L. no. 104-104, 110 stat. 56, http://transition.fcc.gov/Reports/tcom1996.pdf.

40 University of California (Santa Barbara), University of North Carolina (Chapel Hill), University of Texas (Austin), and University of Wisconsin (Madison), *National Television Violence Study, Scientific Papers 1994–1995* (Studio City, CA: Mediascope, 1995). See also the important annual reports to US Congress by the UCLA Center for Communication Policy (from 1994–95, 1995–96, and 1996–97), referred to online at http://www.cbsc.ca/english/links/otherdocs.php.

41 CBSC, "History of AGVOT and Rating Classifications in Canada," http://www.cbsc.ca/english/agvot/aboutagvot.php.

42 CRTC, "Blocking Features and Parental Control," last modified 22 December 2008, http://www.crtc.gc.ca/eng/info_sht/b314.htm.

43 Ultimately, in TQS re The Movie L'inconnu (Never Talk to Strangers) (CBSC Decision 98/99-0176), 23 June 1999, the CBSC extended the application of the watershed requirement for the broadcast of violent content intended exclusively for adults to sexual, coarse language, and other mature content of a corresponding level, despite the fact that the language of the Violence Code had not changed. Ultimately, the expanded watershed application was reflected in the 2002 amendments to the CAB Code of Ethics (clause 10).

44 CRTC, "Violence on TV," 12 August 2008, http://www.crtc.gc.ca/eng/info_sht/b317.htm.

45 CRTC, Broadcasting Public Notice CRTC 1996-134, Revised Timetable for the Implementation of the Television Program Classification System and V-chip Technology, 4 October 1996.

46 CBSC, "Ratings Classifications," http://www.cbsc.ca/english/agvot/ratings.php.

47 Manufacturers voluntarily integrated the V-chip; Canadian legislation or regulations did not require them to do so.

48 Submission of the Canadian Broadcast Standards Council to the Standing

Committee on Canadian Heritage regarding Bill C-327, 6 March 2008, 3.

CHAPTER FIVE

1 Criminal Code of Canada, s. 406A, added by An Act to Amend the Criminal Code, S.C. 1914, c. 24, s. 1.
2 Combines Investigation Act, s. 33C, added by An Act to Amend the Combines Investigation Act and the Criminal Code, S.C. 1960, c. 45, s. 13.
3 Transferred from the Criminal Code to the Combines Investigation Act as s. 33D by the Criminal Law Amendment Act, S.C. 1968-69, c. 38, s. 116. It was renumbered as s. 37 in the R.S.C. 1970, c. C23.
4 Ibid., s. 36(1).
5 Competition Act, R.S.C. 1985, c. C-34, s. 74.01.
6 ASC, Canadian Code of Advertising Standards, http://www.adstandards.com/en/standards/cancodeofadstandards.aspx.
7 Consumer Protection Act, L.Q. 1971, c. 74, s. 102(o).
8 Ibid., s. 11.53(*n*).
9 *Attorney General (Que.) v. Kellogg's Co. of Canada et al.*, [1978] 2 S.C.R. 211, http://scc.lexum.org/en/1978/1978scr2-211/1978scr2-211.html.
10 McGrath was then a member of the House of Commons Standing Committee on Broadcasting, Television, Films and Assistance to the Arts, and was later that lieutenant governor of Newfoundland and Labrador from 1986 to 1991.
11 Consumer Protection Act, S.Q. 1978, c. 6.
12 The act was now R.S.Q., c. P-40.1 and the relevant sections of the Regulation Respecting the Application of the Consumer Protection Act, R.R.Q., c. P-40.1, r. 1, are s. 87 to 91 in division II of chapter VII, entitled "Advertising Directed at Children."
13 *Quebec (Attorney General) v. Irwin Toy Limited*, [1989] 1 S.C.R. 927, http://scc.lexum.org/en/1989/1989scr1-927/1989scr1-927.html.
14 Ibid., 987.
15 Regulation Respecting the Application of the Consumer Protection Act, R.R.Q. 1981, c. P-40.1, r.1, s. 91.
16 The prohibition of broadcasting advertising messages during children's programs includes "the time periods immediately preceding and immediately following [programs], which are not part of the preceding or following programs," in OPC, *Application Guide for Sections 248 and 249 of the Quebec*

Consumer Protection Act (Advertising for Children Under 13 Years of Age) (29 September 1980), 2098(d).

17 Ibid., 2098(c).

18 "The percentages pertaining to the proportion of viewers aged 2 to 11, and to which this guide refers, are based on the Bureau of Broadcast Measurement (BBM) figures." Ibid., 2098(d).

19 Ibid. Note that there is a useful, but not identical, brochure published by the OPC entitled *Your Kids and Ads*, 2009, http://www.opc.gouv.qc.ca/Documents/Publications/SujetsConsommation/FinancesAssurances/PubliciteTrompeusePratiques/EnfantsPub/EnfantsPub_En.pdf.

20 CBC, "Programming not Eligible for Commercial Content," in CBC Program Policy No. 11, 17 December 1996.

21 Pierre Trudel, "La réglementation de la publicité audiovisuelle au Canada et aux Etats-Unis," in Charles Debbasch and Claude Gueydan, *Publicité et audiovisuel* (Paris: Presses universitaires d'Aix-Marseille, Économica, 1993).

22 CBC, "Commercial Impact" (24 September 2002) in CBC Program Policy 1.1.10, paragraph 6(c).

23 ASC, Canadian Code of Advertising Standards, http://www.adstandards.com/en/standards/cancodeofadstandards.aspx.

24 ASC, "The Code," Broadcast Code for Advertising to Children, http://www.adstandards.com/en/clearance/childrens/broadcastcodeforadvertisingto children-thecode.aspx.

25 ASC, "Ad Complaints Report Archive," http://www.adstandards.com/en/standards/previousreports.asp.

26 S. 1(c).

27 ASC, "Broadcast Code for Advertising to Children – Guidelines and Procedures," http://www.adstandards.com/en/clearance/childrens/broadcastcodeforadvertisingtochildren-guidelinesandprocedures.aspx.

28 ASC, "Interpretation Guideline #2 – Advertising to Children," s. 2.2(a), http://www.adstandards.com/en/standards/interpretingthecode.aspx.

29 CAB, "Advertising to Children in Canada: A Reference Guide," May 2006, http://www.cab-acr.ca/english/social/advertisingchildren/kids_reference_guide.pdf.

30 Ibid., 5.

31 CMA, Code of Ethics and Standards of Practice, http://www.the-cma.org/regulatory/code-of-ethics.

32 CCA, "Mission and Mandate," last modified 2010, http://www.cca-kids.ca/english/about_cca/mission_mandate.html.

33 CCA, "Public Service Announcements," http://www.cca-kids.ca/english/psas/index.html.

34 Our translation.

35 CQPP, "Coalition québécoise sur la problématique du poids," *Complaints Lodged*, http://www.cqpp.qc.ca/en/advertising-to-children/complaints-lodged.

36 ASC also has guidelines concerning the sale of products forbidden to minors. For further details, see Code of Advertising Standards, s. 5.1.3.

37 Pursuant to the Importation of Intoxicating Liquors Act, R.S.C. 1985, c. I-3.

38 Canada Revenue Agency, "A Win for Wine! Bill C-311 Receives Royal Assent," 28 June 2012, http://www.cra-arc.gc.ca/nwsrm/rlss/2012/m06/nr120628b-eng.html.

39 Although provincial laws also apply, we will not discuss them here.

40 CRTC, Code for Broadcast Advertising of Alcoholic Beverages, in CRTC Circular No. 329, "Requirements regarding the Review of Broadcast Advertising of Alcoholic Beverages," 23 January 1987.

41 Composed of CBC, CAB, and Health Canada representatives, this committee helps the CRTC analyze advertising messages.

42 CRTC, Code for Broadcast Advertising of Alcoholic Beverages, 1 August 1996, http://www.crtc.gc.ca/eng/general/codes/alcohol.htm.

PART TWO

1 Motion Picture Association of America, *Theatrical Market Statistics 2011*, http://www.mpaa.org/resources/93bbeb16-0e4d-4b7e-b085-3f41c459f9ac.pdf.

2 Statistics Canada, *Household Equipment, 1997 to 2007*, http://www41.statcan.gc.ca/2009/40000/tbl/cybac40000_2009_000_t08-eng.htm.

CHAPTER SIX

1 Canadian Film and Television Production Association (now the Canadian Media Production Association), *The Guide 2009–2010* (Toronto, 2009).

2 These studios are Universal, Warner Bros, Paramount, 20th Century Fox, Sony, and Walt Disney.

3 MPA Canada, "The Logos and What They Mean," http://www.mpa-canada.org/?q=content/logos-and-what-they-mean.

4 Ibid.

5 Cinema Act, R.S.Q., c.C-18.1.

6 Ibid., s. 1.

7 Ibid., s. 86.2.

8 According to the Régie, "by 'public order' is meant respect for society and for the safety and well-being of those who constitute it," and "by 'good morals' is meant the set of commonly held rules governing human behaviour, what a society recognizes generally as good or evil." Régie du cinéma du Québec, *Film Classification in Quebec* (1992), 20.

9 Regulation Respecting Licences to Operate Premises Where Films Are Exhibited to the Public, Distributors' Licences and Video Material Retail Dealers' Licences, O.C. 743-92, 20 May 1992, G.O.Q. 1992.II.2745.

PART THREE

1 Entertainment Software Association of Canada, *Essential Facts about the Canadian Computer and Video Game Industry* (2010), 4.

CHAPTER SEVEN

1 In 1995, Sega of Canada Inc also asked the CRTC for permission to provide a video game service to cable subscribers. The CRTC agreed, but under certain conditions. For further information, see "The Pay Television and Pay-per-View Programming Code regarding Violence" in chapter 4 of this volume.

2 Some of the inconsistencies were noted in Herbert N. Foerstel, *Free Expression and Censorship in America: An Encyclopedia* (Westport: Greenwood Press, 1997), 223.

3 Further details regarding the rating board history can be found on the SegaRetro website at http://segaretro.org/entertainment_software_rating_board.

4 ESRB, "Frequently Asked Questions," http://www.esrb.org/ratings/faq.jsp.

5 ESRB, "Game Rating and Descriptor Guide," http://www.esrb.org/ratings/ratings_guide_print.jsp.

6 ESRB, "Retail Partnership Programs," http://www.esrb.org/retailers/index.jsp.

7 Retail Council of Canada, "Commitment to Parents," http://www.retailcouncil.org/advocacy/national/issues/cp/ctp.

8 Entertainment Software Association, "2010 Sales, Demographic and Usage Data: Essential Facts about the Computer and Video Game Industry," 15, http://www.theesa.com/facts/pdfs/esa_essential_facts_2010.pdf.

9 Ontario Film Review Board, "Video and Computer Game Update," 14 March 2005, http://www.ofrb.gov.on.ca/english/page19.htm.

10 Government of Manitoba, *Manitoba Culture, Heritage, Tourism and Sport, Annual Report 2007–2008*, http://www.gov.mb.ca/chc/reports/pdf/2007_08_ar.pdf.

11 Government of Saskatchewan, "New Legislation Regulates Video Games," 21 March 2006, http://www.gov.sk.ca/news?newsid=5ee97e8a-ee11-455b-9b7a-0ceb54767599.

12 Film and Video Classification Act, S.A. 2008, c. F-11.5, http://www.qp.alberta.ca/1266.cfm?page=F11P5.cfm&leg_type=Acts&isbncln=9780779737444; see also the Alberta Film Ratings website, http://www.albertafilmratings.ca/act/default.aspx.

13 Régie du cinéma du Québec, *My Child and the Screen*, Quebec, 2009, 67, http://www.rcq.qc.ca/guide_mon-enfant_2_en.pdf.

PART FOUR

1 Statistics Canada, *Individual Internet Use and E-commerce*, 12 October 2011, http://www.statcan.gc.ca/daily-quotidien/111012/dq111012a-eng.htm.

2 Statistics Canada, *Canadian Internet Use Survey*, 2009, http://www.statcan.gc.ca/daily-quotidien/100510/dq100510a-eng.htm.

3 For further details, see "The Future Environment Facing the Canadian Broadcasting System," part 8.1.1.

4 Charles Zamaria, Fred Fletcher, and André H. Caron, *Canada Online! A Comparative Analysis of Internet Users and Non-users in Canada and the World: Behaviour, Attitudes and Trends 2004*, October 2005, http://www.canadianinternetproject.ca/en/docs/canadaonlinefinalenglishversion10302005.pdf.

5 Charles Zamaria and Fred Fletcher, *Canada Online! Year Two Report, 2007*, September 2008, http://www.omdc.on.ca/assetfactory.aspx?did=6324.

6 *Canada Online!*'s 2007 survey sample did not include the six-to-eleven age group.

7 Réjean Roy, CEFRIO, *Génération C: Les 1224 ans* (Moteurs de transformation des organisations, December 2009).

8 Internet World Stats, "Stats," http://www.internetworldstats.com/stats.htm.

CHAPTER EIGHT

1 CRTC, Telecom Public Notice CRTC 99-14 and Broadcasting Public Notice CRTC 1999-84, New Media, 17 May 1999.

2 Ibid., s. 122.

3 CRTC, Broadcasting Public Notice CRTC 1999-197, *Exemption Order for New Media Broadcasting Undertakings*, 17 December 1999.

4 CRTC, "New Media Project Initiative," 4 June 2009, http://www.crtc.gc.ca/eng/media/media3.htm.

5 CRTC, *Perspectives on Canadian Broadcasting in New Media,* 2008, http://www.crtc.gc.ca/eng/media/rp080515.pdf.

6 Ibid.

7 CRTC Broadcasting Regulatory Policy 2009-329, Review of Broadcasting in New Media, 4 June 2009.

8 Ibid.

9 *Reference re Broadcasting Act*, [2012] 1 S.C.R. 142.

10 Industry Canada, *Illegal and Offensive Content on the Internet* (Ottawa, 2000), 5, http://publications.gc.ca/collections/collection/c2-532-2000e.pdf.

11 Samuel Perreault, "Self-Reported Internet Victimization in Canada, 2009," *Statistics Canada*, 15 September 2011, http://www.statcan.gc.ca/pub/85-002-x/2011001/article/11530-eng.htm.

12 The Senate Standing Senate Committee on Human Rights, "Senate Committee on Human Rights to Conduct Study on Cyber-Bullying Committee Committed to Issues Affecting Youth," 12 December 2011, http://www.parl.gc.ca/content/sen/committee/411/ridr/press/12dec11-e.htm.

13 Standing Senate Committee on Human Rights, *Cyberbullying Hurts: Respect for Rights in the Digital Age* (2012), http://www.parl.gc.ca/content/sen/committee/411/ridr/rep/rep09dec12-e.pdf.

14 Commission d'accès à l'information du Québec, *Rapport quinquennal 2011: «Technologies et vie privée à l'heure des choix de société»* (Commission d'accès à l'information du Québec, 2011).

15 Resolution proposed at the 30th International Conference of Data Protection and Privacy Commissioners in Strasbourg in 2008, https://www.priv.gc.ca/information/conf2008/res_cop_e.asp,

16 Office of the Privacy Commissioner, *Annual Report to Parliament 2010: Personal Information Protection and Electronic Documents Act*, June 2011.

17 G. Sinclair, G.J. Zilber, and E. Hargrave, *Regulating Content on the Internet:*

A New Technological Perspective (Industry Canada, March 2008), http://www.ic.gc.ca/eic/site/smt-gst.nsf/eng/sf09058.html#s5.

18 Ibid.

19 D. Goetz and G. Lafrenière, "Bill C-15A: An Act to Amend the Criminal Code and to Amend Other Acts," 12 October 2001 (revised 30 September 2002), http://www.parl.gc.ca/about/parliament/legislativesummaries/bills_ls.asp?ls=c15a&parl=37&ses=1.

20 *R. v. Sharpe*, [2001] 1 S.C.R. 45, http://scc.lexum.org/en/2001/2001scc2/2001scc2.html.

21 Goetz and Lafrenière, "Bill C-15A."

22 Ibid.

23 L. Casavant and J.R. Robertson, *The Evolution of Pornography Law in Canada*, 25 October 2001, http://www.parl.gc.ca/Content/LOP/ResearchPublications/843-e.htm.

24 Ibid.

25 Cybertip.ca, "About Us," http://www.protectchildren.ca/app/en/ctip.

26 RCMP, "Internet Security," last modified 29 December 2011, http://www.rcmp-grc.gc.ca/qc/pub/cybercrime/cybercrime-eng.htm.

27 Ibid.

28 Ibid.

29 Canadian Association of Broadcasters, *Advertising to Children in Canada: A Reference Guide*, May 2006, http://www.cab-acr.ca/english/social/advertisingchildren/kids_reference_guide.pdf.

30 CMA, Code of Ethics and Standards of Practice, http://www.the-cma.org/regulatory/code-of-ethics.

31 Canadian Association of Internet Providers, "Supporting the Government of Canada's 'Strategy on Illegal and Offensive Content on the Internet: Promoting Safe, Wise and Responsible Internet Use': CAIP's Largest Members Do Their Part," April 2002, http://www.cata.ca/files/PDF/caip/Big-Members-brochure.pdf.

32 Government of Canada, *Illegal and Offensive Content on the Internet*, 1999, http://publications.gc.ca/collections/collection/c2-532-2000e.pdf.

33 Canadian Association of Internet Providers, "Supporting the Government of Canada's 'Strategy on Illegal and Offensive Content on the Internet,'" 1–2.

34 Canadian Association of Internet Providers, "CAIP's Internet Tips for Parents," 31 August 2000, http://www.cata.ca/files/pdf/caip/caip-tips1.pdf.

35 Canadian Association of Internet Providers, "CAIP Children's Online Pledge," 31 August 2000, http://www.cata.ca/files/pdf/caip/caip-childs pledge.pdf.

36 Canadian Association of Internet Providers, "Code of Conduct," http://www.cata.ca/files/pdf/caip/caip_code_of_conduct.pdf.

37 Its initial survey (2001), Phase II (2005), and Phase III (2012) can be found online at http://mediasmarts.ca/research-policy.

38 MediaSmarts also conducted qualitative interviews with key informant teachers in February and March of 2011. See *Young Canadians in a Wired World, Phase III – Teachers' Perspectives*, 2012, http://mediasmarts.ca/research-policy for a detailed report of its findings.

39 MediaSmarts, *Young Canadians in a Wired World, Phase III – Teachers' Perspectives*.

40 MediaSmarts, *Young Canadians in a Wired World, Phase III – Talking to Youth and Parents about Life Online*, 2012, http://mediasmarts.ca/sites/default/files/pdfs/publication-report/full/YCWWIII-youth-parents.pdf.

41 YMA, "About YMA," http://www.ymamj.org/a_propos_en.html.

42 Centre for Youth and Media Studies, *A National Study on Children's Television Programming in Canada*, 2010, http://www.ymamj.org/pdf/nationalstudy.pdf.

43 Sonia Livingstone et al., *EU Kids Online*, September 2011, http://www2.lse.ac.uk/media@lse/research/eukidsonline/eu%20kids%20ii%20(2009-11)/eukidsonlineiireports/final%20report.pdf.

44 World Internet Institute, 2009.

45 Sonia Livingstone and R. Das, *Existential Field 8: Media, Communication and Information Technologies in the European Family* (European Commission, 2010), 10.

46 Insafe, *Insafe Annual Report: Promoting Safe and Responsible Use of Online Technology* (2011), 19, http://www.saferinternet.org/c/document_library/get_file?uuid=30208e01-2459-4646-830f-5053f5f990f5&groupId=10137.

47 Council of Europe, "Council Recommendation on the Development of the Competitiveness of the European Audiovisual and Information Services Industry by Promoting National Frameworks Aimed at Achieving a Comparable and Effective Level of Protection of Minors and Human Dignity," *Official Journal of the European Union*, OJ L 270 (7 October 1998).

48 "Recommendation 2006/952/EC of the European Parliament and of the Council of 20 December 2006 on the Protection of Minors and Human

Dignity and on the Right of Reply in Relation to the Competitiveness of the European Audiovisual and on-line Information Services Industry," *Official Journal of the European Union*, OJ L 378 (27 December 2006).

49 "Directive 2007/65/EC of the European Parliament and of the Council of 11 December 2007 Amending Council Directive 89/552/EEC on the Coordination of Certain Provisions Laid down by Law, Regulation or Administrative Action in Member States Concerning the Pursuit of Television Broadcasting Activities," *Official Journal of the European Union*, OJ L 332 (18 December 2007), 27–45.

50 Council of Europe, "Convention on Cybercrime," Budapest, ETS no. 185 (23 November 2001), http://conventions.coe.int/treaty/en/treaties/html/185.htm.

51 Council of Europe, "Convention on the Protection of Children against Sexual Exploitation and Sexual Abuse," Lanzarote, CETS no. 201 (25 October 2007), http://conventions.coe.int/treaty/en/treaties/html/201.htm.

52 Council Framework Decision 2004/68/JHA on Combating the Sexual Exploitation of Children and Child Pornography, *Official Journal of the European Union*, OJ L 013 (20 January 2004), 44–8, http://eur-lex.europa.eu/lexuriserv/lexuriserv.do?uri=oj:l:2004:013:0044:0048:en:pdf.

53 Council Framework Decision on Combating the Sexual Abuse, Sexual Exploitation of Children and Child Pornography, Repealing Framework Decision 2004/68/JHA. Brussels, 25 March 2009, 2009/0049 (CNS), http://www.statewatch.org/news/2009/jun/eu-council-trafficking-9892-09.pdf.

54 Decision 276/1999/EC of the European Parliament and of the Council of 25 January 1999 adopting a Multiannual Community Action Plan on Promoting Safer Use of the Internet by Combating Illegal and Harmful Content on Global Networks, *Official Journal of the European Union*, OJ L 33 (6 February 1999), 1, http://eur-lex.europa.eu/lexuriserv/lexuriserv.do?uri=oj:l:1999:033:0001:0011:en:pdf.

55 European Commission Information Society, "Safer Internet Programme: Empowering and Protecting Children Online," http://ec.europa.eu/information_society/activities/sip/index_en.htm.

56 European Commission Information Society, "Empowering and Protecting Children Online," February 2009, http://ec.europa.eu/information_society/doc/factsheets/018-safer-internet.pdf.

57 Europe Commission Information Society, "Safer Internet Programme."

58 Insafe, *Insafe Annual Report: Promoting Safe and Responsible Use of Online Technology*, 2011, http://www.saferinternet.org/c/document_library/get_file?uuid=d169d15e-eb88-4423-9b1f-17b8d13784b4&groupid=10145.

59 European Commission Information Society, "Mobile Operators Agree on How to Safeguard Kids Using Mobile Phones," 6 February 2007, http://ec.europa.eu/information_society/newsroom/cf/itemlongdetail.cfm?item_id=3153.

60 GSMA Europe, "European Framework for Safer Mobile Use by Younger Teenagers and Children," 2009, http://serving.webgen.gsm.org/5926da9a-2dd6-48e7-bad4-50d4cd3af30a/assets/safer_mobile_flyer.pdf.

61 Ibid.

62 GSMA Europe, "European Framework for Safer Mobile Use."

63 European Commission, "Social Networking: Commission Brokers Agreement among Major Web Companies," 10 February 2009, http://ec.europa.eu/information_society/newsroom/cf/itemlongdetail.cfm?item_id=4672.

64 European Commission Information Society, "Safer Social Networking Principles for the EU," 2009, https://ec.europa.eu/digital-agenda/en/safer-social-networking-principles-eu.

65 Until the Ofcom amalgamation, responsibility for broadcasting matters lay in the hands of the Broadcasting Standards Commission and the Independent Television Commission. Together with the Office of Telecommunications, the Radio Authority, and the Radiocommunications Agency, it became Ofcom in December 2003.

66 In October 2011, it assumed responsibility for the postal service industries from the Postal Services Commission.

67 Ofcom, UK Code of Practice for the Self-regulation of New Forms of Content on Mobiles, 11 August 2008, http://stakeholders.ofcom.org.uk/market-data-research/media-literacy/archive/medlitpub/ukcode and http://stakeholders.ofcom.org.uk/binaries/research/media-literacy/ukcode.pdf.

68 European Commission Information Society, "European Framework for Safer Mobile Use by Younger Teenagers and Children," http://ec.europa.eu/information_society/activities/sip/self_reg/phones/index_en.htm.

69 ASA, "History of Ad Regulation," http://www.asa.org.uk/regulation-explained/history-of-ad-regulation.aspx.

70 Ibid.

71 Committee of Advertising Practice, "Advertising Codes," http://www.cap.org.uk/advertising-codes.aspx.

72 Ibid., general section 5.

73 Internet Watch Foundation, "About Us," http://www.iwf.org.uk/about-iwf.

74 Aviva Gutnick, M. Robb, L. Takeuchi, and J. Kotler, *Always Connected: The New Digital Media Habits of Young Children* (New York: The Joan Ganz Cooney Center at Sesame Workshop, 2010).

75 V.J. Rideout, U.G. Foehr, and D.F. Roberts, *Generation M^2: Media in the Lives of 8- to 18-Year-Olds* (Menlo Park: Henry J. Kaiser Family Foundation, 2011), 16.

76 Ibid.

77 Federal Communications Commission, "What We Do," http://www.fcc.gov/what-we-do.

78 Actually Title V of the Telecommunications Act of 1996, P.L. No. 104-104, 110 stat. 56 (1996), the indecency provisions of the CDA were struck down by the United States Supreme Court in *Reno v. American Civil Liberties Union*, (1997), 521 U.S. 844. See also the *Congressional Research Service Report for Congress: The Communications Decency Act of 1996* by Henry Cohen, online at http://www.ipmall.info/hosted_resources/crs/96-321.pdf.

79 Children's Online Privacy Protection Act, 15 U.S.C. s. 6501–6508.

80 Federal Trade Commission, "Frequently Asked Questions about the Children's Online Privacy Protection Rule," accessed 19 March 2012, http://www.ftc.gov/privacy/coppafaqs.shtm.

81 The Do Not Track Kids Act, H.R. 1895, 112th Cong. (2011–2012).

82 15 U.S.C. §§ 6501-6506 (Pub. L. 105-277, 112 Stat. 2581-728, enacted 21 October 1998).

83 Federal Communications Commission, "Children's Internet Protection Act Guide," 19 May 2011, http://www.fcc.gov/guides/childrens-internet-protection-act.

84 Danah Boyd et al., "Why Parents Help Their Children Lie to Facebook about Age: Unintended Consequences of the 'Children's Online Privacy Protection Act,'" *First Monday* (16): 11, 7 November 2011.

85 The Family Online Safety Institute, "About ICRA," http://www.fosi.org/icra.

86 ESRB, "Websites Certified by ESRB Privacy Online," last modified 28 August 2012, http://www.esrb.org/privacy/sites.jsp.

87 ESRB and CTIA – The Wireless Association, "CTIA – The Wireless Association and ESRB Announce Mobile Application Rating System," 29 November 2011, http://www.esrb.org/about/news/downloads/ctia_esrb_release_11.29.11.pdf.

88 CARU, "Self-regulatory Program for Children's Advertising," http://www.caru.org/guidelines/guidelines.pdf.

89 Ibid.

90 Federal Trade Commission, "The Children's Advertising Review Unit Self-Regulatory Guidelines for Children's Advertising," http://www.ftc.gov/privacy/safeharbor/caruselfreg.pdf.

91 Federal Trade Commission, "Interagency Working Group Seeks Input on Proposed Voluntary Principles for Marketing Food to Children," last modified 28 April 2011, http://www.ftc.gov/opa/2011/04/foodmarket.shtm.

92 American Academy of Pediatrics, "Current Published Policy Statements/ Clinical Reports," http://www2.aap.org/sections/media/resources.cfm#policy.

93 L. Green, D. Brady, K. Ólafsson, J. Hartley, and C. Lumby, *Risks and Safety on the Internet for Australian Children: Full findings from the AU Kids Online Survey of 9–16 Year Olds and their Parents* (ARC Centre of Excellence for Creative Industries and Innovation, 2011).

94 ACMA, "The ACMA Overview," http://www.acma.gov.au/web/standard/pc=acma _org_oview.

95 Internet Industry Association, icode, http://iia.net.au/userfiles/iiacyber securitycode_implementation_dec2010.pdf.

96 ACMA, "What is Cybersmart?" http://www.cybersmart.gov.au/about%20cyber smart/what%20is%20cybersmart.aspx.

97 "How to complain about children and the media," http://childrenandmedia .org.au/taking-action/how-to-complain.

CONCLUSION

1 CRTC, Broadcasting Public Notice CRTC 1996-36, Policy on Violence in Television Programming, 14 March 1996.

2 Kaiser Family Foundation, *Parents, Children and Media: A Kaiser Family Foundation Survey*, June 2007, http://www.kff.org/entmedia/upload/7638.pdf.

3 See CRTC, "Results of the Fact-Finding Exercise on the over-the-top Programming Services," October 2011, http://www.crtc.gc.ca/eng/publications /reports/rp1110.htm, and the follow-up commission letter of 12 April 2012, reaffirming the CRTC's initial finding, at http://www.crtc.gc.ca/eng/archive /2012/lb120416.htm.

Index